RUGBY

St

D

Nat

Human Kinetics

WOODRIDGE PUBLIC LIBRARY
3 PLAZA DRIVE
WOODRIDGE, IL 60517-5014
(630) 964-7899

Library of Congress Cataloging-in-Publication Data

Biscombe, Tony, 1945–
    Rugby : steps to success / Tony Biscombe, Peter Drewett.
      p.   cm.
    Includes bibliographical references (p.)
    ISBN 0-88011-509-2
    1. Rugby Union football.   I. Drewett, Peter, 1958–   .
  II. Title.
  GV946.2.B57   1998
  796.333--dc21   97-29732
                                                 CIP

ISBN: 0-88011-509-2

Developmental Editor: Kirby Mittelmeier; **Managing Editor:** Jennifer Stallard; **Editorial Assistants:** Jennifer Hemphill and Laura Seversen; **Copyeditor:** Karen Bojda; **Proofreader:** Erin Cler; **Graphic Designer:** Keith Blomberg; **Graphic Artist:** Kathleen Boudreau-Fuoss; **Cover Designer:** Jack Davis; **Photographer (cover):** Tom Roberts/Human Kinetics; **Illustrator:** John Hatton; **Mac Art:** Jennifer Delmotte; **Printer:** Versa Press

Instructional Designer for the Steps to Success Activity Series: Joan N. Vickers, EdD, University of Calgary, Calgary, Alberta, Canada

Human Kinetics books are available at special discounts for bulk purchase. Special editions or book excerpts can also be created to specification. For details, contact the Special Sales Manager at Human Kinetics.

Printed in the United States of America   10 9 8 7 6 5 4 3 2

Human Kinetics
Web site: http://www.humankinetics.com/

United States: Human Kinetics, P.O. Box 5076, Champaign, IL 61825-5076
1-800-747-4457
e-mail: humank@hkusa.com

Canada: Human Kinetics, 475 Devonshire Road, Unit 100, Windsor, ON N8Y 2L5
1-800-465-7301 (in Canada only)
e-mail: humank@hkcanada.com

Europe: Human Kinetics, P.O. Box IW14, Leeds LS16 6TR, United Kingdom
+44 (0)113-278 1708
e-mail: humank@hkeurope.com

Australia: Human Kinetics, 57A Price Avenue, Lower Mitcham, South Australia 5062
(08) 82771555
e-mail: humank@hkaustralia.com

New Zealand: Human Kinetics, P.O. Box 105-231, Auckland Central
09-523-3462
e-mail: humank@hknewz.com

CONTENTS

FOREWORD

If ever a book was well timed it is Steps to Success—Rugby Union. Since the game became a professional sport in 1995, players have become fitter, stronger and more skilful, and this has led to fast, open, dynamic rugby—everything a spectator wants to see.

The skills now required to succeed in Rugby Union need constant practice, and authors Tony Biscombe and Peter Drewett have based the techniques shown in this book on a wealth of coaching and teaching experience at all levels in the game.

The practices and drills are game related and have achievable outcomes. Players are encouraged to learn through creative and innovative situations which challenge their previous experience and knowledge.

The book recommends effective practice of playing techniques in a safe environment, and also provides the individual player with a range of challenging self-test drills to check for improvement in skill levels. By keeping a record of these achievements the player is able to chart a progress up the Steps to Success Staircase.

Player development is the key to team success. This book stimulates players and coaches alike, by providing enjoyable practice situations, based on sound educational principles. By using the authors' ideas, you will see major gains in skill levels, and improvement in performance by players, units and team.

Don Rutherford
Director of Rugby
Rugby Football Union

PREFACE

Understanding and achieving success in the game of rugby union often takes a number of years. Success in the game is rather like the flights of a spiral staircase. Once you reach the top of one level on the staircase, you may have to go on to another one in order to improve. Sometimes when you have reached the top of the second level, you will need to revisit the first one in order to refine and polish your skills.

This book attempts to highlight the basic skills required by all players and some of the more important technical skills needed for the different positions in the team. There are many skills for you to practise, and the book contains a number of drills so that your practice is worthwhile, structured and focused. Many of the practices are used frequently by the best players, and you should never lose sight of the fact that your level of skill can be improved by constant, purposeful repetition. Your aim at every training session should be to achieve the best possible practice.

Rugby union provides you with many challenges. It will challenge your commitment, bravery, judgment and physical ability. These challenges increase as you grow older; it is only by constantly testing yourself and re-evaluating your current ability that you will constantly improve as a player.

Many people have helped in the production of this book: our long-suffering wives, Larraine and Felicity, who endure many hours alone at home with our children while we are away watching, coaching and lecturing on this great game but who always give their full support and backing to our activities; our colleagues in the Technical Department of the Rugby Football Union, who have inspired so many excellent ideas; and our personal assistants, Dee Horsley and Penny Bishop, who helped and encouraged us. There are many other people who should receive some acknowledgment, but it is impossible to list them all. However, one person more than any other has inspired us: Chalkie White, in our opinion the most accomplished coach of his era and one of the great thinkers about the game of rugby union. To him we both owe a great deal, and we thank him for his advice, encouragement and inspiration over the past few years as both colleague and friend.

THE STEPS TO SUCCESS STAIRCASE

The staircase to success in rugby union is one that leads off in many directions. As with most spiral staircases, it branches off partway to the top, and it is up to you to choose the direction you wish to continue to climb.

On the first few steps up the staircase, you will learn the skills important for all players and how to practise them so that you improve. You should familiarise yourself with these first sections before you begin to specialise and climb the spiral staircase of technical skills.

You should follow the same sequence on each step of the staircase, starting with practices with no pressure and gradually increasing until your technique, performed against full opposition, becomes a skill. At the same time you must be aware of and follow the information given to you on essential equipment and how to prepare your body to play a contact sport.

As you climb the steps to rugby success, follow the same sequence for each step:

1. Read the explanations of what the step covers, why the step is important and how to execute the step's focus, which might be a basic skill, concept, tactic or combination of all three.

2. Follow the numbered illustrations showing exactly how to position your body to execute each basic skill successfully. There are three general parts to each skill description: preparation (getting into the right position), execution (performing the skill that is the focus of the step) and follow-through (finishing position).

3. Look over the common errors that might occur and recommendations for how to correct them.

4. Read the directions, the Success Goals and the Success Check items for each drill. Practise accordingly and record your scores and improvement. You need to meet the Success Goal(s) for each drill before moving on to practise the next one, because the drills are arranged in an easy-to-difficult progression. This sequence of drills is designed specifically to help you achieve continued success. Pace yourself by adjusting the drills to either increase or decrease their difficulty, depending on your skill level.

5. As soon as you can reach all the Success Goals for one step, you're ready for a qualified observer, such as your teacher, coach or trained partner, to evaluate your basic skill technique against the Keys to Success found at the beginning of each step. This provides a qualitative, subjective evaluation of your basic technique. By focusing on correct technique, you can enhance your performance. Ask your observer to suggest improvements.

6. Repeat this procedure for each of the 11 Steps to Success, then rate yourself according to the directions for "Rating Your Progress".

In the early steps many of the Success Goals are measured in the number of repetitions you can perform consecutively before the skill breaks down. As you work up the staircase, you will find more and more opposition is introduced, and success becomes rather more difficult to define. For example, tries are sometimes scored from 90 metres out from the goal line: This is success for those players involved in carrying the ball over that distance, but success may also be measured rather differently. If you are the first player close to your own goal line who sees the gap in the defence and makes the pass that puts your team's try makers beyond the defence, that is your success. The try makers themselves may pull the remaining defence to one side in order to give the try scorer the final pass—that is their success. The try scorer's success is in finishing the movement and collecting the points for the team.

When learning a new skill, check the Keys to Success found at the beginning of each step. You might ask a teammate or the coach to observe your early attempts at the skill and to check your positioning, foot position or body movement, for example, against the illustrations and explanations of the technique. Some of the advanced technical skills require a very experienced observer to help you achieve success in these early stages. As you progress up the staircase, you will find that achieving the Success Goals becomes easier because you have been constantly refining your skills.

As you move from those steps associated with basic skills into the more specialised areas, you should begin to rate your progress on the charts provided. If you add the date to your rating and constantly update the chart, you will have an idea of whether or not you are improving your skills. It is always a good idea to have an experienced observer also check your rating so that you have the opportunity to discuss your progress.

As with most staircases, the rugby Steps to Success are climbed many times in a lifetime. The time you spend revisiting the first few steps will never be wasted in rugby union. Even the most successful international rugby players climb the steps of basic skills three or four times each week. These skills are the foundation upon which all else is built, and you must climb the staircase regularly in order to improve.

By planning your journey up the staircase carefully, you will learn new skills that you can take to the game of rugby union. The most successful teams are often those that involve all 15 players in a journey up a staircase of success, which ultimately leads to open, exciting and skilful rugby union.

THE GAME OF RUGBY UNION

In the early years of rugby in the 19th century, the game was played primarily by the great public schools, who played it for recreation. Many schools had their own sets of rules, but in nearly every case the ball was both handled and kicked, and only the method of scoring changed from place to place.

By 1845 the game was already very well established, and the first set of "Laws of Football" was produced at Rugby School in England. The game in those days was far less complicated than today. It had many differences from the modern game but also some similarities, and a number of modern terms already existed, for example, offside, knock-on, try and touch.

In those days no player was allowed to play until he had been awarded his cap, and this is thought to have been the precedent for the awarding of caps at the international level. The length of match varied, but a match could have been played for a number of afternoons over an extended period of time, with over 50 players on unequal sides. Eventually numbers were reduced to 20 a side, and ultimately to 15.

The rugby game you now play was largely developed from the actions of a schoolboy named William Webb Ellis. He died in 1872, the year after the formation of the Rugby Football Union and the adoption of the laws of Rugby School. He is buried in Menton, France, and his grave is cared for by local rugby enthusiasts. Little could Webb Ellis have known that his actions would ultimately create an organised world-wide game enjoyed by thousands of players and watched by huge numbers of spectators at live matches and on television. A stone has been erected at Rugby School to honour Webb Ellis; it reads: "This stone commemorates the exploit of William Webb Ellis, who, with a fine disregard for the rules of football as played in his time, first took the ball in his arms and ran with it, thus originating the distinctive feature of the rugby game. AD 1823". The World Cup has been named the Webb Ellis Trophy in recognition of the schoolboy from Rugby School.

The original rugby ball was a pig's bladder inside a leather casing. When inflated, the bladder formed an oval shape. Nowadays this shape is reproduced by ball manufacturers using modern materials.

Rugby has become a way of life for people throughout the world where the game is played. A World Cup competition every four years has given rugby an even greater international identity, and the number of people playing the game continues to increase. Indeed, the International Rugby Football Board has appointed an officer to oversee the funding and development of rugby in emerging nations. Currently over 70 countries have an international rugby team.

How Rugby Union Is Played

The laws of the game of rugby football state: "The objective of the game is that two teams of fifteen players each, observing fair play according to the Laws and a sporting spirit, should by carrying, passing, kicking and grounding the ball score as many points as possible, the team scoring the greater number of points to be the winner of the match". While this describes the game in a nutshell, there are many laws, and it will take time for you to learn all of them. The laws of rugby are amended and developed by the International Rugby Football Board (IRFB). The IRFB constantly reviews and, when necessary, changes laws to help players to enjoy a safer and more exciting game. These Laws are to be found in the Book of Laws produced by the International Rugby Football Board and the Rugby Unions of each playing member of the international community.

Before a game starts, the team captains meet to toss a coin, and the visiting captain calls. The winner of the toss can choose to kick off or to receive kick-off and defend a particular goal line for the first half. Captains often will choose a particular end because of weather conditions; for example, the wind or bright sun might give your team an advantage. The game starts with a kick-off (place kick) at the centre of the half-way line, and the ball must reach your opponents' 10-metre line.

The side who gain possession must attempt to work the ball down to their opponents' goal line by running, passing the ball sideways or backward or kicking the ball. If one team manages to carry the ball over the goal line and place it down, a try is scored (currently worth 5 points). That team then has the opportunity to kick a goal in line from where the try was scored (currently worth 2 points). The game restarts back at the half-way line with another kick.

If the ball goes over the sidelines (touch lines), the game is restarted with a line-out (refer to Step 7). For handling infringements a scrum (refer to Step 7) brings the ball into play, and for offences against an opponent the referee may award either a free kick or penalty. Points may be scored from penalties by kicking the ball over the crossbar of the posts (currently worth 3 points). Anyone in position on the field may also drop kick the ball over the crossbar to score points (currently worth 3 points). The game is normally played outdoors on grass, although it may also be played on clay or sand if it is not dangerous. Diagram 1 shows the markings and dimensions of the playing area for the 15-per-side game.

Once the ball is in play, each player has a part to play in the game. Everyone should be a good ball handler, tackler and runner. Although most positions have a specialist role when the game is restarted, the best teams contain individuals who have excellent overall skills.

The IRFB recommends names for each player position and for the numbers worn by each. Different countries, however, have a variety of names for playing positions (see glossary). Diagram 2 shows the numbers and playing positions of a team at a scrum situation.

At senior and international levels, a game of rugby lasts for 80 minutes. It is split into two playing periods of 40 minutes, with a half-time interval of 5 minutes. During the interval players rest, have a drink, talk tactics and change ends.

One of the best rugby laws, which makes rugby different from other games is advantage, which can override a number of other laws but not those which cover foul play. "When the result of an infringement by one team is that their opponents gain an advantage, the referee shall not whistle immediately for the infringement." The purpose of the advantage law is to make play more continuous as a result of fewer stoppages for transgressions. You should encourage your team to "play to the whistle" despite infringements by your opponents, because this often results in your team's scoring. The advantage can be tactical (a good attacking opportunity) or territorial (a gain in ground).

When rugby first began to be played, captains acted as referees and made decisions during the game. There has always been a great emphasis on fair play in rugby. Perhaps that is why you can travel the world and always receive a fine welcome in any rugby club.

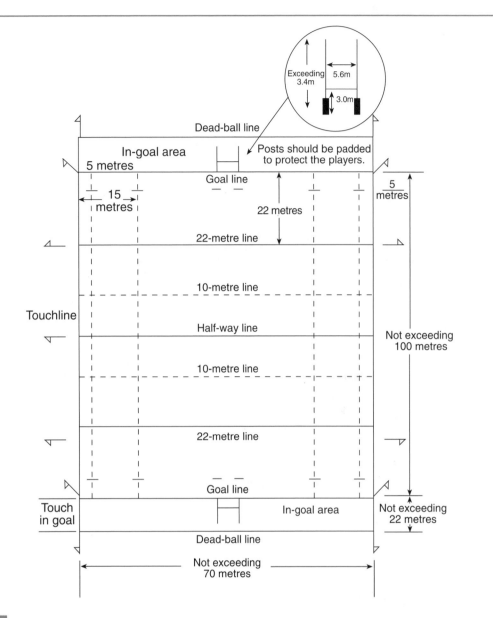

Exceeding 3.4m

5.6m

3.0m

Dead-ball line

In-goal area
5 metres

Posts should be padded
to protect the players.

Goal line

15
metres

22 metres

22-metre line

10-metre line

Touchline

Half-way line

10-metre line

Not exceeding
100 metres

22-metre line

Goal line

Touch
in goal

In-goal area

Not exceeding
22 metres

Dead-ball line

Not exceeding
70 metres

5
metres

Diagram 1 Markings and dimensions of the playing area for the 15-per-side game.

You will make a lot of lifelong friends playing rugby. You are now part of the ever-increasing rugby family.

Rugby is a game for the whole family. It is played by people of both sexes and all ages, sizes, shapes and abilities. Tournaments and matches are arranged for 6-year-olds to veterans with certain law variations to help everyone play safely. For example, non-contact, two-handed touch rugby or tag rugby (where the removal of a ribbon signals a tackle) can be played by people of all ages for recreational fun or competitively in organised leagues.

Most rugby-playing countries acknowledge that young players are better off learning the game by playing in teams of fewer than 15 a side to give players more opportunities to touch the ball and participate in the game. As a result, variations and modifications of the

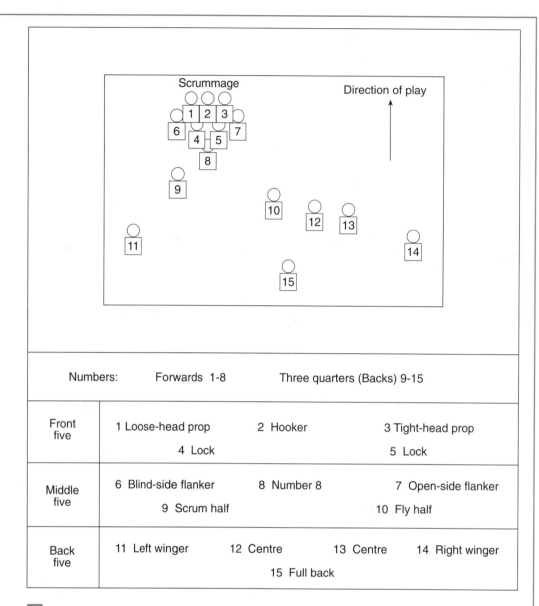

Numbers:	Forwards 1-8	Three quarters (Backs) 9-15

Front five	1 Loose-head prop	2 Hooker	3 Tight-head prop
	4 Lock		5 Lock
Middle five	6 Blind-side flanker	8 Number 8	7 Open-side flanker
	9 Scrum half		10 Fly half
Back five	11 Left winger 12 Centre	13 Centre	14 Right winger
	15 Full back		

■ **Diagram 2** Numbers and playing positions of a team at a scrum situation.

senior game have been recommended for young players. The following table shows examples of recommended variations for different age groups.

Preparing to Play

You may try to avoid contact as much as possible while you are playing, but nevertheless there will be times when you will collide with members of the opposition, members of your own team or the ground. Under no circumstances, therefore, should you take the field physically under-prepared for these collisions.

In your late teenage years, you might consider using a weight-training schedule to build up the strength and power required to play against other adults, but in your early teenage years, you should exercise using only your own body weight as the resistance. An overall

Table 1				
Age group	Pitch size	Number in team	Ball	Duration of play
Under 7 & 8	30 m × 20 m	5-7	3	2 × 10 min
Under 9 & 10	50 m × 35 m	9 (3 forwards & 6 backs)	3	2 × 10 min (< 9), 2 × 15 min (< 10)
Under 9 & 10	50 m × 35 m	9 (3 forwards & 6 backs)	3	2 × 10 (U9), 15 (U10) mins
Under 11	59 m × 38 m	9 (3 forwards & 6 backs)	3	2 × 15 min
Under 12	59 m × 43 m	12 (5 forwards & 7 backs)	4	2 × 20 min
Under 12	59 m × 43 m	12 (5 forwards & 7 backs)	4	2 × 20 mins
Under 14	Usually smaller than full size	15 (8 forwards & 7 backs)	4	2 × 25 min
Under 15	Usually smaller than full size	15 (8 forwards & 7 backs)	5	2 × 30 min
Over 15	Full size	15 (8 forwards & 7 backs)	5	2 × 35 min
Over 19	Full size	15 (8 forwards & 7 backs)	5	2 × 40 min

strengthening programme initially will be quite sufficient. However, different playing positions make different strength demands. For example, the strength required of a prop is not the same as that of a winger. To build up further strength in your body, you should take part in body-weight circuits. On occasions you may wish to use a partner's body weight as the resistance, but your own is often quite sufficient. You might also consider wrestling for the ball against a partner or working with a heavy tackle bag that you repeatedly drive into, lift and throw to the ground. All these actions are very similar to those you do in the game.

Because of the nature of the game and the rough and tumble that characterises it, there are occasions when each of the joints of your body will come under extreme force and will be moved through a wide range of movement even if you do not want them to be. There will be no problem with injury if you have followed a daily flexibility regime that has helped to stretch muscles and extend the range of your joints. However, before any exercise, including rugby practice, you must follow a warm-up and stretching routine to help prepare your body for exercise.

Warm-Up

Warm-up is exactly what the name suggests: increasing the body's temperature to prepare it for vigorous exercise. Wear warm clothing to begin with. To begin, jog for a short period of time to raise your body temperature, go into your routine of stretches and finish with a further jog to raise your temperature even further. If you feel any tightness in any of your muscles, those muscles should be stretched again after the second jog. Remember your sequence of stretches and follow it during warm-up.

There are a number of golden rules when stretching that you should always adhere to.

Stretch only after you have raised the temperature of your body. This is not achieved by sitting next to a radiator, but by exercising gently for a short period of time. Under no circumstances should you bounce up and down in your stretch position. This kind of ballistic stretching is highly dangerous and can cause injury.

All stretches should be applied firmly and gradually to the point of full stretch. The fully stretched position should be held for approximately 10 to 20 seconds. After 10 seconds you should find that the stretched muscles begin to automatically relax and any tension begins to disappear. It is at this point that you begin to increase the range of movement in the area being stretched. As you release the stretch, it often helps to shake the muscle gently to release any residual tension.

You should always follow a systematic stretching routine. Work from one end of the body to the other in sequence: for example, from ankles up to neck, or down the other way, or from the large abdominal muscles outward.

After the Match or Training

After playing or training, it is a good idea to go through a number of cool-down stretches to help avoid stiffness in the muscles. You should follow the same sequence as in your warm-up stretches. Drink water or a sports drink immediately after the match to rehydrate and replenish your carbohydrate stocks. Eating a banana is also an ideal after-match or after-training snack, as bananas are packed with easily accessible carbohydrates. This should help you to recover more quickly from the strenuous activity.

Check to see if you have any lumps, bumps or grazes. Small lumps and bumps can be easily reduced by the application of ice, wrapped in a thin towel or inside a plastic bag. Any grazes or small cuts should be cleaned with an antiseptic, and dressings applied as required. Any severe swelling or pain in and around joints should be checked by the medical team.

Always bathe or shower, not only for cleanliness, but also to invigorate you and help you relax and recover.

Personal Equipment

There are many situations in training and playing that can cause a slight injury. You should therefore take the precaution of wearing the safety equipment allowed in laws of the game (see figure 1). The use of light shin pads to protect your shins is a must, especially for the front five forwards, though all players benefit from using them. Every player on your team should be fitted with a gum shield. A gum shield helps to protect your teeth and jaw and often prevents concussion if there is a clash of heads. Gum shields that are not fitted by a dentist should be avoided, as they are easily dislodged in contact.

Simple protective horseshoe strapping on your ankles prevents injury. No other strapping should be considered. If you need heavy strapping on any part of the body, you should not play. By playing with an injury, you risk making that injury much worse. An extra week away from the game is a far better option for you.

Make sure that you are always up to date with a preventive course of tetanus injections to help prevent serious infections in even the slightest of wounds.

As you prepare for a match, you should adopt good habits. Always pack your kitbag the night before you are due to play. Make sure everything in your kit is clean, and check laces for fraying. Pack your tie-ups for your socks and your protective equipment (shin pads and gum shield). Check for any excessive wear on your studs, and if necessary replace them with new ones. Make sure you understand all meeting arrangements for the pregame period so that you can arrive promptly. Lateness is a very bad habit and cuts down on the time you have to prepare mentally and physically for vigorous exercise.

Remember to clean your boots after the match if the ground was muddy, so that the leather can dry out. This will help your feet to breathe during the next match. If you are still stiff the day after a game, you might try gentle exercise such as swimming or riding a cycle to help remove the stiffness.

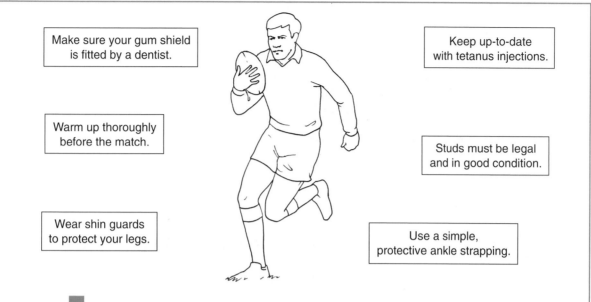

Make sure your gum shield is fitted by a dentist.

Warm up thoroughly before the match.

Wear shin guards to protect your legs.

Keep up-to-date with tetanus injections.

Studs must be legal and in good condition.

Use a simple, protective ankle strapping.

Figure 1 Safety equipment allowed in laws of the game.

You now know some of the history and traditions of the game of rugby union football and also how to begin to prepare yourself to play the game. Once you have the basic equipment, it's time to begin your journey on the Steps to Success staircase.

Key			
●	Attacker	→	Direction of run attack/defence
○	Defender	■	Marker
⇢	Direction of pass or kick	◓	Ruck/maul
	Player kneeling with outstretched arm		Player holding tackle shield
	Step sequences/foot positions		Areas to attack/defend
	Scrum		Direction of push in scrum
	Player in scrum		Tackle bag
	Line-out		Marker flag
	Rugby ball		

STEP 1

BALL HANDLING: MAINTAINING POSSESSION STARTS HERE

All rugby players need good ball-handling skills to cope with the different demands of the attacking game: running with the ball, passing and catching at pace (at actual game speed). Great teams have players who take the fullest advantage of attacking situations; to do this they must keep possession of the ball. To truly succeed as a rugby player, you must be skilful in executing the basic ball-handling techniques and drills in this chapter.

The position you may play in the future is of little importance in comparison to your overall range of skills, of which ball handling is part. The drills and practices shown in this step are designed to help you develop basic ball-handling techniques that you will use in the changing situations in a game.

During play the ball may arrive at different angles, heights, speeds and forces. A ball that arrives at a difficult angle may affect your ability to keep possession. For example, a pass that arrives from behind at knee height may be difficult to catch and bring to your waist while you are running at pace and attempting to maintain balance. Becoming used to the unique shape of the ball early on will give you confidence and help you to cope with the unexpected when it happens—such as a ball bouncing wildly off the turf or a pass thrown too high or away from you.

The modern approach to the game is to try to retain possession for as long as possible. Often this task must be performed while in contact with the opposition. The ball-handling drills shown in this first step will help your chances of retaining possession in close-contact situations.

When practising basic ball-handling techniques, it's important to practise with a ball that is the right size for your hands so that it is easy to grip.

How to Handle the Ball

It is to your advantage whenever possible to carry the ball in two hands. This allows you to either pass or keep the ball safe when a tackler grabs hold of you. It also allows you to make a more accurate pass in open play. When holding or moving the ball around your body, grab it firmly in your hands with your fingers spread across the seams. The seams will help you maintain your grip. Use your fingers to control the ball, not your palms. Figure 1.1 shows a proper grip.

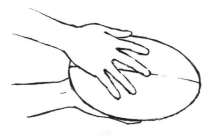

Figure 1.1 Use your fingers to control the ball.

Often a ball carrier will hold the ball along his or her forearm or tuck it into the ribs near the elbow when running in the open field. This is a safe carrying style and allows you to run more quickly because you can pump your arms with the running motion. However, by tucking the ball, you make it difficult to readjust the ball in order to pass. When you run with the ball tucked in, you must always be prepared to readjust your grip to pass with two hands on the ball.

DRILLS

1. Around Your Body

Stand with your feet shoulder-width apart, with the ball held in two hands at waist level out in front, fingers spread across the seams of the ball. Move the ball clockwise around your body, changing hands from front to back, and then counter-clockwise. Begin slowly; as you achieve success, gradually speed up. Always try to move your body in rhythm with the pace and movement of the ball and reach for the ball as far around your body as you can. Always keep the ball off the palms of your hands; it is your fingers that control and grip the ball. Also try to keep the ball away from your clothing so that you do not drop it.

Success Goal = 10 times clockwise around your body without dropping the ball; 10 times counter-clockwise ___

Success Check
• Reach for ball behind back ___
• Extend fingers across seams of ball ___

To Increase Difficulty
• Move ball faster around your body.
• Increase number of repetitions.
• Use a larger ball.
• Walk with eyes closed.
• Walk forward slowly, gradually increasing speed.

To Decrease Difficulty
• Use a small, round ball.
• Slow down the movement.

2. Figure 8 Juggling

This is a great drill that allows you to combine movement with ball-handling practice.

a. Stand with feet slightly farther apart than your shoulders and legs bent slightly at the knee. Bend over at the waist, keeping your back as flat as possible. Hold the ball in two hands, with your fingers spread across the seams and away from your body in front. Move the ball around and behind one of your legs with one hand, passing it between your legs around to the other hand in the front. Allow your body to sway with the movement of the ball. Repeat the movement around the back of the other leg and between your knees, finishing with the ball in front. The ball will have followed a figure 8.

b. Once you have mastered the figure 8 juggle, you should try it as you walk. At first you may want to lift your leg a bit to allow the ball to pass under, but this will make it extremely difficult to walk, especially as you may need to take much longer strides to make space for the ball to pass under the legs. Try first to walk normally and at a good pace while moving the ball around your knees; then try to increase your speed to a jog.

Success Goals =

a. 10 successful figure 8s to the left; then 10 to the right ____

b. Walk over a 10-metre distance while constantly moving the ball; then jog the same distance ____

Success Check

- Concentrate on moving ball smoothly ____
- Spread fingers across seams ____
- Allow body to sway sideways with movement of ball ____
- Walk or jog normally with slightly longer strides ____

To Increase Difficulty

- Move the ball as quickly as possible at the edge of control.
- Close your eyes while moving the ball.
- Reverse the direction of the movement so that you move the ball behind your knee first.

To Decrease Difficulty

- Use a smaller ball.
- Make all movements slowly.

3. Under Your Leg

Stand with your feet shoulder-width apart. Hold the ball in two hands away from the body, arms straight. Lift one leg, bending it at the knee. Pass the ball from one hand to the other around the outside of your thigh and under the lifted leg. Lower that leg, raise your other leg and repeat by passing the ball around the other leg. Aim for developing a smooth movement involving both legs.

Success Goal = 10 circular movements around each leg ____

Success Check

- Spread fingers wide along seams of ball ____
- Lift leg as ball moves across front ____

To Increase Difficulty

- Walk forward, and lift your knee high as you pass the ball under each leg in turn.
- Reverse direction, moving the ball from inside and under your leg to the outside.

To Decrease Difficulty

- Use a smaller ball.

4. Around Your Head and Body

Here's another ball-handling drill that allows you to practise moving the ball while changing body positioning.

a. Stand with your feet shoulder-width apart, ball in both hands, arms bent so that the ball is at head height. Pass the ball around your head from one hand to the other at about ear height. Make sure the ball doesn't roll against or otherwise touch your head and that the ball passes from one hand to the other in front and then behind your head.

b. When you can successfully perform the movement around your head, it is time to move the ball up and down your body. Stand with your feet close together, ball held in both hands, fingers spread across the seams, slightly out in front of you. Pass the ball first around your head, then around your waist, down behind your knees, and finish around your ankles.

Success Goals =
a. 10 times clockwise around head, 10 times counter-clockwise; 5 times in one direction, then 5 in the other ____
b. One successfully completed movement from head to ankles; then one from ankles to head ____

✔ Success Check
• Spread fingers along seams of ball ____
• Do not allow ball to touch clothing or body ____

To Increase Difficulty
• Close your eyes.
• Walk forward and gradually increase speed until you can jog while moving the ball.
• Stand up and sit down continuously while you pass the ball around your head.
• Speed up the movement of the ball.
• Start from your head, go down to your ankles, and return to your head.

To Decrease Difficulty
• Use a smaller ball.
• Slow down your movements.

5. Between Your Knees

Stand with your feet slightly wider than shoulder-width apart, knees slightly bent. Bend forward at the waist. Hold the ball between your knees with your left hand behind you and your right hand at the same height in front. Hold the ball with the fingers spread across the seams. Keep your hands relaxed. Try to exchange the positions of your hands, letting go of the ball and switching hands from front to back, without allowing the ball to drop to the ground. Begin slowly and gradually increase your speed. Stay relaxed; don't rush.

Success Goal = 5 successive catches; then 30 seconds of successful catching ___

Success Check
- Hold ball with tips of fingers ___
- Do not snatch at ball ___
- Relax while moving hands ___

To Increase Difficulty
- Widen your stance and speed up your hand movements.

To Decrease Difficulty
- Just before you let go of the ball, straighten your legs slightly so that the ball lifts. Then bend them as you catch the ball. As you work, your hips move up and down.

6. Catch Above Your Head

With this drill you'll be able to start focusing on simple catching movements.

a. Stand with your feet shoulder-width apart, ball held in two hands out in front of the body. Throw the ball up above your head, watching it as it flies. Allow both hands to follow the ball so that your fingers point at it. As the ball falls, spread all your fingers. As it touches your fingers pull it down in both hands and in to your lower chest area, keeping your elbows close to your ribs.

b. Sometimes in a match—especially if you've misjudged a kick or there is a wind blowing—you may have to turn to catch the ball. Once you can successfully complete the previous throwing and catching sequences, you should begin to practise throwing the ball above your head and turning to face in a different direction to catch it.

Hold the ball in two hands in front of the body. Throw the ball above the head and slightly over one shoulder. Watch the flight of the ball closely and turn your body so that your chest is facing the falling ball, but keep your feet still. Catch the ball with palms of hands facing you, hands slightly higher than your eyes. As the ball touches your fingers, pull it in to your lower chest, elbows tucked into ribs.

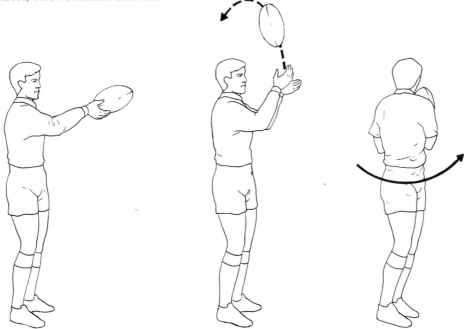

After you can do this successfully, throw the ball higher and slightly farther from the body. In order to catch now you will need to turn not only your chest, but also your feet so that you turn round to face the ball as it drops.

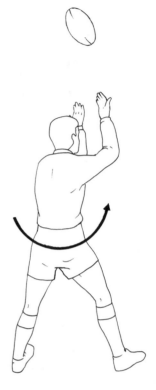

As you master the turn and catch, repeat the drill with a jump, turn and catch; there are many situations in a match that demand this skill. Always make sure to time your jump so that you catch the ball in the air and finish in a safe squat position, ball tucked firmly to your lower chest area.

Success Goals =
a. 10 consecutive catches in place ___
b. 5 consecutive catches while turning ___

Success Check
- Watch the ball ___
- Tuck elbows into ribs ___
- Pull ball to chest, cradling it firmly in hands and arms ___

To Increase Difficulty
- Throw the ball 3 times and clap before each catch.
- Increase the number of times you throw, clap and catch until you can do it successfully for 1 minute.
- Try to clap twice before each catch.
- Throw a little higher, touch your hips, clap and then catch.
- Throw, touch your knees, touch your hips, clap and catch.
- Finally, throw, touch ground, touch knees, touch hips, clap and catch.
- Jump to catch after turning through a full circle.

To Decrease Difficulty
- Touch only one place (e.g., ground, knees or hips) before catching the ball.
- Throw the ball higher to allow time for your turn.

7. Catch Behind Your Back

Stand with your feet shoulder-width apart, knees slightly bent. Throw the ball just over your head, and catch it behind your back at waist height. Remain upright as you catch, watch the ball until it goes over your head. Avoid bending forward when making the catch; if you do, the ball will roll down your back and you will drop it.

Success Goal = 15 successful consecutive catches ___

Success Check
• Watch ball as long as you can ___
• Move hands quickly behind you and spread fingers wide ___
• Do not bend forward ___

To Increase Difficulty
• Once you have caught the ball, throw it back over your head and catch it. Throw by flicking your wrists and fingers upward and bending your arms quickly from the elbows.

To Decrease Difficulty
• Throw the ball lower, just over your head.

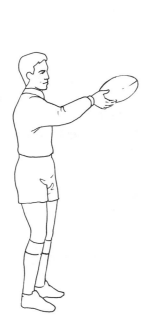

8. Catch Over Your Shoulder

There are many occasions in games when the ball is passed slightly too far in front or behind you, and you will have to turn to collect it or try to catch it in an awkward way. This drill helps you practise these techniques. The variations simulate catching the most awkward of passes that may be fired at you. Remember to practise in both directions.

To practise collecting a ball that has been passed just behind you, throw it from your waist, over one shoulder, move your hands quickly to behind turning at the waist to catch the ball.

Now throw the ball over your left shoulder, turn to the right at the waist and catch it on your right hip. Then try it to the left. Put only enough power in the throw for the ball to clear your shoulder. Although your arms will move with the ball, flick your fingers and wrists in the direction you want the ball to go. As you pass over your shoulder, turn your body as far round as possible before you release the ball.

Success Goals =
a. 10 successful catches over each shoulder ___
b. 10 successful catches alternating shoulders ___

Success Check
- Watch ball as long as possible ___
- Move hands quickly ___
- Throw just clears shoulder ___
- Spread fingers wide, palms toward ball ___

To Increase Difficulty
- Walk backward slowly.
- Walk forward slowly.

To Decrease Difficulty
- Throw the ball a little higher than your head.

BALL-HANDLING SUCCESS SUMMARY

While there are many other skills you must learn to become a good rugby player, ball handling is a very important piece in the puzzle of skills needed. To improve, you must spend a great deal of time with the rugby ball in your hands. Make up your own ball-handling exercises and drills. It's a fun and useful way to practise new skills. Quality practice helps make quality rugby players.

STEP 2

PASSING AND RECEIVING: GAINING THE ATTACKING EDGE

Rugby union is a game of running and ball movement, so you will need to become expert at sending the ball to other members of your team while on the move. Teams that have players who pass well will cause their opponents many defensive problems.

Accurate, early passing prevents the defence from dominating the attack. By constantly moving the point of the attack, the defence will find it impossible to become set. Teams that play like this need to be very fit, because there is little opportunity for rest by attackers and defenders. The ball is continually passed away from would-be tacklers, so the passing team needs many players running in support of the ball carrier. The main purpose of this strategy is to make the attack so overpowering that at some stage there will be more attackers in one area than there are defenders. With accurate passing and receiving, the attacking team can strike around the edge or through the defence to score.

When you are running close to tacklers, it is safest to carry the ball in two hands slightly out in front of the chest. From this position it is possible to make most passing movements. This position helps protect the ball when one of the defenders tries to tackle you. At other times, when you are running in open space, you can hold the ball along one forearm tucked to your lower rib area. This position helps keep you in balance when running at top speed.

There are only three types of passes in the game: the lateral pass, which travels sideways or backward; a switch pass, which changes direction of the play; and a loop pass, which helps to put a player either through a gap in the defensive line or into space around the far edge of the defence (overlap). In this chapter we look at these passing skills. There are a number of other passes (e.g., gut pass, screen pass, etc.) which are simply slightly different ways of making lateral passes. For more about passing the ball in contact situations, see Step 6.

Making Effective Passes

A good pass has a number of requirements—accuracy is perhaps the most important. Sometimes you may be required to pass with power and other times softly. It is far better to pass with too little rather than too much power. A soft pass will draw the receiver toward the ball. This will help keep the attack moving toward the goal line lines, the defence will be unable to drift across to the edge of your attack, and therefore space around the edges of the defence will be maintained for the next attempt at a score. A powerful pass often pushes the receiver away from the most effective running line, which is normally parallel to the touch line. Your receiver may be forced to run slightly sideways, which makes tackling by the defence easier and the attack less likely to penetrate or overlap the opposition because it lessens the space outside the edge of the defence. Once you can control the power of your pass, you will begin to send out passes that will allow other players to make best use of the available attacking options.

The height at which the passed ball arrives is crucial. If it arrives below chest height, the receiver will have to look down to catch it. This means that the player will look away from the defence and may lose sight of an attacking opportunity. Passing too high has the same effect and will also expose the receiver's ribs to a hard tackle. The ideal pass arrives at about chest height, with enough power (whether soft or hard) to allow the receiver to play to the best advantage of the team.

Although there are only three basic passes, there are various ways to pass the ball. All involve some movement of the arms, wrists and fingers. A short, punched lateral pass may require just a strong flick of the wrists and fingers. For long passes you may need to use the full swing of your arms and also of larger parts of your body, such as shoulders, hips and legs.

There are no right or wrong ways to pass the ball. You may have already developed a style that allows you to send out accurate passes that you can easily vary in height, length and power. If not, then try different techniques during practice sessions. Once you find a style that suits you, it is correct. Your main concern is to develop a technique that allows you to send accurate passes that vary in length, height, power and direction.

Passing Situations

During play there will be many opportunities for attacking players to create space for support players to run into. The task of the attackers nearest the space is to recognise it in advance or to create situations in which the attack outnumbers the defence: two attackers versus one defender or three attackers against two defenders and so on. A key ingredient of success in these passing situations is to draw the defenders toward you—committing them to tackling you—to create space for another attacker to push through (see diagrams 2.1 and 2.2). The drills in this chapter will help you to practise these skills. As you develop your passing game, you should seek to create and take advantage of these situations.

When practising passing and receiving skills, defensive players should use two-handed touch tackling, touching the ball carrier on the hips with both hands instead of full contact tackling. This technique allows players to refine passing skills under defensive pressure without exposing them to injury.

How to Execute the Lateral Pass

To move the ball up the field, you can run in any direction, but you may pass the ball only sideways or backward. Therefore the lateral, or sideways, pass is the basic pass.

Sometimes a pass travels a short distance, at other times much farther. Sometimes it is a soft pass that

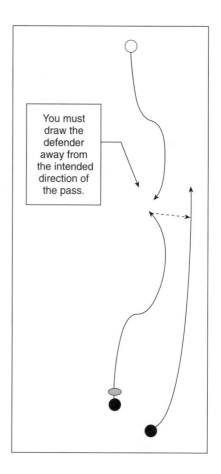

You must draw the defender away from the intended direction of the pass.

Diagram 2.1 Draw the defender toward you.

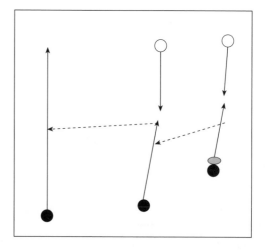

Diagram 2.2 Create space for the extra defender.

floats toward the receiver, but on other occasions it may travel much farther, spinning with great power and speed as it arrives in the player's hands. No matter which kind of pass you send, there are a number of basic techniques that you should remember for the lateral pass.

Always try to pass the ball with two hands. Spread your fingers around the seams, keeping your palms away from the surface of the ball. Carry the ball at chest height when you are ready to pass, but also practise passing the ball from different heights—for example, near the knees or above the head—so that you are prepared for any eventuality in the game.

When you prepare to pass, you must decide how far, at what height and how powerfully the ball should be sent to determine your passing action. For short, soft (pop) passes, hold the ball at chest height and flick the fingers and wrists slightly upward toward the receiver (see figure 2.1c). This type of pass can also be used if you pick up a rolling ball and wish to flick it on to another player. For slightly longer passes,

which you might make when you are running as an attacking line, you need only to extend the action further by allowing your arms to move further across your body toward the receiver.

For passes that miss out (skip over) players running in the line, you may have to swing your shoulders and turn at the waist to add more power (see figure 2.1b-c). Sometimes you may want a pass to travel over a long distance and arrive as quickly as possible. To do this the ball must spin point first, rather like a bullet. The easiest way to spin the ball is for the hand behind the ball to push toward the receiver and then quickly move up the side and over the top of the ball. Your other hand guides and grips the ball. In all cases your hands and fingers must complete the follow-through and finish pointing at the intended target (see figure 2.1a-c).

FIGURE 2.1 | **KEYS TO SUCCESS**

LATERAL PASS

  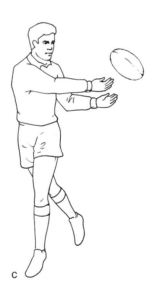

a   b   c

Preparation

1. Ball in both hands, only fingers in contact ___
2. Carry at chest height ___
3. Look at opponent ___
4. Then look at receiver as you prepare to pass ___
5. Choose speed, direction, height, distance and power ___

Execution

1. Swing arms toward receiver ___
2. Push ball with rear hand ___
3. Guide ball with other hand ___
4. Flick wrists and fingers as ball leaves hands ___

Follow-Through

1. Watch ball as it leaves hands ___
2. Point fingers at target area ___
3. Change running angle and follow ball to support new ball carrier ___

How to Execute the Switch Pass

There are times in a match when the defence is tight and your attack is running out of space. To confuse the defence or to create a little more space, you might consider using a switch pass. This pass can quickly change the direction of an attack or hide the ball for a split second from the defence so that you create a little time or space before the defence responds.

To execute the switch pass you must first run as a threat to a defender. Once the defender begins to follow your running line and you are closing toward each other, you alter your running line to go across that of the receiver (see figure 2.2). As you and the receiver cross close together, turn at the waist with the ball toward the receiver behind you, look at the receiver's hands and softly flick the ball up into the space in front of the receiver's hands (see figure 2.2). A gently lobbed, soft pass will allow the receiver to accelerate into the ball and at the same time keep the defence in sight. Once you have passed the ball, you must work hard to rejoin the attack as a support runner, even though you initially may be running away from the direction of the next ball carrier.

FIGURE 2.2

KEYS TO SUCCESS

SWITCH PASS

Preparation

Ball carrier:
1. Ball in both hands, only fingers in contact ___
2. Carry at chest height ___
3. Threaten the defender ___
4. Quickly change running angle to go between defender and receiver ___

Receiver:
1. Make a target ___
2. Watch defender and ball carrier ___
3. Accelerate as ball is passed ___

Execution

Ball carrier:
1. Deliver soft, lobbed pass up in front of target ___
2. Turn as you pass so that ball is hidden from defender ___

Follow-Through

Ball carrier:
1. Run to support new ball carrier ___

For the switch pass to be successful, it's important that the ball always be visible to the members of your own team, especially to the player who is going to receive the pass. If you are running to the right you will turn around with the ball behind your right hip; if you are running to the left, it will be behind your left hip (see diagram 2.3).

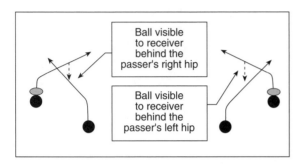

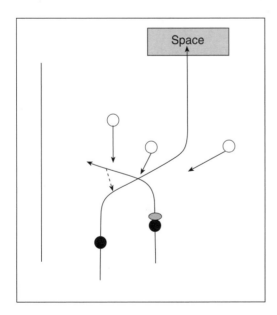

Diagram 2.3 The ball is visible to players in your team.

A switch pass is normally used to redirect the attack parallel to the touch lines, to put a player back at an angle to a defence that is running across the field (see diagram 2.4), or to change the direction of the attack (see diagram 2.5).

Diagram 2.4 Player is back at an angle to the defence.

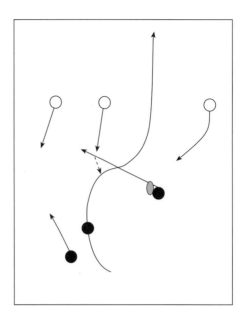

Diagram 2.5 Changing the direction of the attack.

How to Execute the Loop Pass

There are only three ways that you can beat the defence. You can go around it (overlap), go through it (penetrate) or go over it (kick). The loop pass is a ploy that allows you either to create an overlap by putting an extra pair of hands in the attack or to put another player into a gap to penetrate the defence.

The loop pass is another version of the standard lateral pass that offers the ball carrier some options. One option is for the ball carrier to pass to the player next in line, then immediately run behind the new ball carrier and re-enter the line to receive a return pass (see figure 2.3). Another option for the ball carrier is to deliberately miss out the next player in line with the pass, so that the third player receives the ball. The middle player then runs behind and outside the new ball carrier to receive a pass.

The loop pass is executed much the same way as the lateral pass, except that the new ball carrier does not pass the ball directly at the looping player, but into the space in front of the gap the looping player is attacking (see figure 2.3). This makes sure that the receiver is brought onto the effective running line and is able to either penetrate the defence or pass out for the overlap.

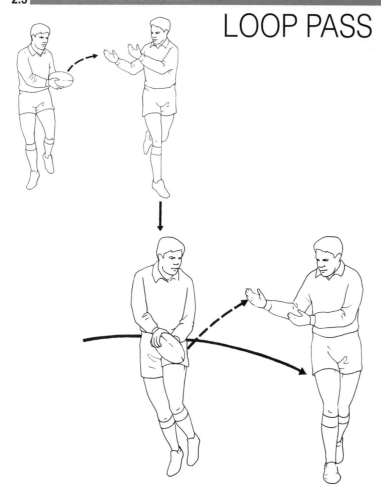

FIGURE
2.3 **KEYS TO SUCCESS**

LOOP PASS

Preparation

1. Ball in both hands, only fingers in contact ___
2. Carry at chest height ___
3. Threaten the defender ___
4. Run slightly inwards towards nearest shoulder to pull defender away from pass direction ___

Execution

1. Receiver makes target ___
2. Watch defender ___
3. Determine length of pass ___
4. Use arms, wrists and fingers to fire pass ___
5. Look at target and pass into gap ___

Follow-Through

1. Make the first pass and then run to support or receive a return pass ___

By running at the defence first, as the ball carrier you will attract a defender toward you and create a gap farther out along the attacking line (see diagram 2.6). If you are the support runner, make sure that you are on your intended running line before you receive the pass (see diagram 2.7). Accelerate as you receive the ball and penetrate the defence (see diagram 2.8).

As with the switch pass, it is possible to use the looping player as a decoy runner by making a dummy pass and then passing to another player in a better position or exchange passes with the ball carrier or pull the last defender towards you and create an overlap for the outside attacker (see diagrams 2.9-2.11).

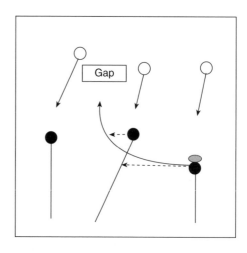

Diagram 2.6 Create a gap farther out.

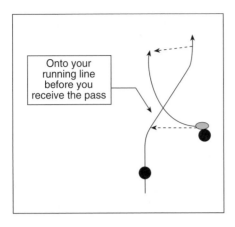

Diagram 2.7   Onto your running line.

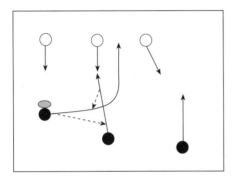

Diagram 2.8   Accelerate and penetrate the defence.

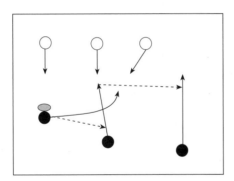

Diagram 2.9   Use the looping player as a decoy.

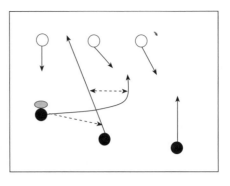

Diagram 2.10   Exchange passes with the ball carrier.

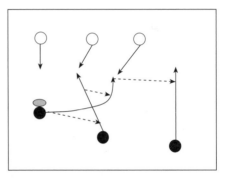

Diagram 2.11   Create an overlap.

Of all the passes you make, the loop gives the greatest range of outcomes. It is a skill that you should try to master as soon as possible. It is effective, however, only if your support players also understand the variations and options. A loop pass is usually a planned move. However, the more you practise with the same players (especially those who play in the positions nearest to yours), the more you will be able to read their body language and instinctively react to them should they improvise and go for the loop.

Practising against a static defence can help you to achieve the timing required to make a successful loop pass; however, the sooner you can advance to a more active defence, the better.

How to Receive a Pass

In a match, attackers with and without the ball must make instant decisions. Ball carriers need to quickly choose the angle at which to run toward the defender, when to pass, the type of pass and how to quickly return to effective support once the pass is completed. Receivers' options are just as varied: They must determine their running angle in relation to the defence and ball carrier, provide a target with hands ready to receive the ball, run in within sight of the ball carrier, determine where the next attack will be and so on.

To receive the ball successfully, you should always make a target with your hands. The best way of providing a target is to hold out your hands toward the passer at about chest height with palms facing the ball (see figure 2.4). The target is then quite easy for the ball carrier to see, and it can also act as a decoy to attract the defender should the ball carrier fake the pass or send out a pass that deliberately misses you out and is collected by the next player in line. The passer should look at the target just before passing and aim the ball so that it will arrive just in front of your hands. Passers should always try to pass from low to high and give sufficient power so that the ball arrives at the target just past the highest point on its trajectory.

Figure 2.4 Make a target.

If the ball is aimed at you, it should arrive just in front of your outstretched fingers so that you can either reach and collect it or accelerate and collect it. In either case you should allow the ball to arrive into your fingers and not the palms of your hands. Your fingers grip the ball naturally, allow you to readjust the ball in your hands if necessary before passing it on, and make it easier for you to pass the ball quickly.

When a ball is arriving from the right, your left hand stops it, and both hands then control it. If you are going to pass it to the left, your right hand pushes it on. For a ball coming from the left, the opposite hands are used.

How to Execute a Dummy Pass

Each of the pass situations described earlier will provide opportunities for you to use a dummy pass. It is best to use a dummy pass when you see that the defender is beginning to take up a running line toward your support player in anticipation of your pass. It is essential that you use the same actions for the dummy as you would when actually intending to pass the ball. This will convince both attacker and defender that you are about to release the ball. At the last moment keep your fingers wrapped around the ball, and bring it back into the carrying position in front of your chest. However, if you always use a dummy pass, you will soon become known for it, and it will cease to be a surprise to the defence. Your attacking options will be therefore diminished.

You can practise the dummy pass in your normal passing drills. Occasionally keep hold of the ball when you see the defender anticipate the pass.

Passing and Receiving Effectively

For the greatest success at passing, you should always keep the ball in front of your body throughout the passing movement. Dragging it around and behind either hip as it is released causes inaccuracy. Turn your chest to face the receiver when passing to a player running 2 or 3 metres behind you. This will allow you to use the same passing technique as normal and should result in an accurate pass.

It's important to practise passes of different lengths when developing your passing skills. As you and your teammates work wider apart, you will find that more and more parts of your body become involved in making the pass. Very short passes will use just the forearms, but long passes will involve arms, shoulders, back and legs. The longer you pass, the more likely that you will be unable to immediately run to support the new ball carrier, because the effort in making the long pass pushes you away from its intended direction.

You will find that swinging the ball with straight arms is not very effective when you and your teammates begin to move much wider apart. Although you use the same pendulum motion for long passes, you now add a flick of the wrists and fingers to pass the ball on to the next player. It also helps if you bend your arms slightly to shorten the length of the swing; this will allow you to use more shoulder and back muscles to add power to the action. Remember to release the ball as your hands begin to travel upward from the bottom of the arc to make sure that the ball is lobbed slightly so that it is just beginning to fall as it nears the target and is therefore easier to catch.

The support runner is not always in the ideal position in a game. You therefore must develop your ability to deliver the ball to either side or to any depth. Your support runner will arrive from different angles and distances. Sometimes you will pass well behind, at other times you may be able to make a flat pass, almost parallel to the goal line. No matter what the situation, you must make sure that your pass arrives safely to the support player.

If you are the support runner, you must select your intended running line before the ball arrives. Good players select one line but run on a slightly different one until the ball is in the air and then change on to the best one very late. This fools the defender and often results in the ball carrier breaking through the defensive line.

When you work against a more active defence, you may find that you have to readjust the timing of your pass. Your coach will tell you when the defence can change from touch to tackle. It may be better if you concentrate on passing rather than tackling for the time being.

PASSING AND RECEIVING SUCCESS STOPPERS

Error	Correction
1. You continually fail to catch the ball.	1. Watch the ball all the way into your hands. Make a target with fingers pointing upward. Close your fingers and thumb around the ball as it arrives.
2. When passing the ball, you cannot seem to hit the target.	2. Follow through after the pass so that your fingers point to the target area. Concentrate on accuracy, not speed.
3. When you try to make a soft pass, it spins quickly toward the receiver.	3. Your rear hand is pushing up and over the top of the ball as you release it. Keep both hands level, fingers pointing to the target.
4. You find it difficult to pass the ball quickly.	4. Catch the ball in the fingers, not the palms of your hands. Flick the ball toward the receiver, using wrists and fingers plus some of the power of your forearms.
5. You always seem to be in front of the passer as the ball is about to be delivered.	5. Keep your depth on the ball carrier. A simple way is to always be able to read the number on the back of his or her shirt. Accelerate only when you see the ball is on its way through the passer's hands.
6. Each time you receive the ball, you lose sight of the nearest opponent.	6. Either your target is too low or your partner is passing the ball below chest height. In both cases, you need to look down for the ball and so lose sight of the defender. Make a higher target for the passer to aim toward.

DRILLS

1. Three in a Line Passing

This drill gets you started with the basic passing motion and provides practice in getting into proper running lines.

a. Practise this drill by walking side by side and close together initially. You must allow your arms to swing while passing the ball. The player on the end has the ball and reaches out with it to the next person, who is close enough to pick the ball out of the ball carrier's hands. In one movement the passer's arms swing the ball down, across and back up into the next pair of waiting hands. Move the ball to the next player as soon as you receive it. Once the ball has gone across the line of players, players pass in the opposite direction and return it to the starting point.

Now, widen the spaces between the players. Start at about 1 metre apart and gradually extend the distance until there is about 3 metres between players. If this distance is too wide, move a little closer. You should not be farther than 3 metres apart until you've mastered this drill.

b. Stand in a line one behind the other with the front person holding the ball. The ball carrier begins to run forward steadily, and the remaining players fan out to one side in an arc, ready to catch and pass. Players behind the ball must work hard to run sideways and then forward onto their running line before receiving the ball.

Success Goals =

a. Walk length of field with no dropped passes, passing in two strides; then run length of field with no dropped passes ___

b. Cover 20 metres 5 times at jogging pace, without stopping or dropping the ball; then at full pace down one edge of playing field, returning to touch line after each successful passing sequence without dropping the ball ___

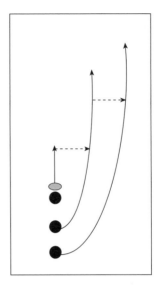

Success Check

• Watch ball into your hands, then turn to look at target ___
• Spread fingers wide across seams, holding ball upright ___
• Use soft passes ___
• Be on intended running line before receiving ball ___

To Increase Difficulty

• Work in 5m channels.
• Try the same exercise with a variety of different balls, such as tennis, basket, hockey, foam, and so on. (Try this also with an egg—it will really help you concentrate on sending the pass to the correct place and on receiving it in the fingers.)
• Use a wider work channel. Front person calls "left" or "right" to decide which way the support runners have to run.

To Decrease Difficulty

• Stay close together.
• Walk steadily and take your time with the pass.
• Walk over short distances, then come back in the opposite direction.
• Shout out the direction before the players begin to run.
• Give the receiver time to run into position before you make the pass.

2. Zigzag Passing

Work in a confined area—no more than a 10-metre square—with two other players. As you continuously jog and change direction, pass the ball to a support player who immediately passes on to the third player. Support players must join the action always from behind but alongside the ball carrier. All potential receivers should show the ball carrier a target and call for the ball. The ball carrier will select which target to hit and should choose the type of pass required to deliver the ball accurately. If the ball comes to you, stop it with one hand and push it across your body with the other one—keep both hands on the ball.

Success Goal = No dropped passes in 30 seconds ___

Success Check

- Follow behind ball carrier until direction changes ___
- Keep eyes on ball ___
- Make a target ___
- Call for the ball ___
- Stop ball movement with hand farthest from direction of pass ___
- Push ball on with other hand ___

To Increase Difficulty

- Change directions while running.
- Make passes as soon as you can after changing direction.
- Add a defender who tries to knock ball to the ground after each pass.

To Decrease Difficulty

- Walk rather than jog.
- Make slower, softer passes that are easy to catch.
- Remove the defender.
- Work along a channel without a change of direction.

3. 2 vs. 1 Passing

Start with a defender about 10 metres away from the ball carrier and a support player directly behind the ball carrier. This distance from the defender will help the support player avoid jogging in front of the ball carrier before the ball carrier is ready to pass the ball.

If you are the ball carrier, your running line should go toward the defender and slightly away from the direction of the pass. Once the defender becomes fully committed to that defensive line, turn to look for your support and get ready to pass the ball as soon as the defender can no longer threaten the receiver.

Remember, it is as important for you to find the support runner as it is for the support runner to catch up to you. If the support runner is not close, either slow down or run across and toward the running line of the defending player.

If you are the pass receiver, you will recognise when the pass is about to be made because the ball carrier will look at you. At that precise moment you make the target and accelerate from behind the ball carrier to collect the pass. The defender will have no chance to tackle you because you take the ball quickly behind the defence.

Allow a number of attempts to beat the defender. Remember to start from different sides of the area you are working in, so that you practise passing to the left and right. After every pass the receiver should try to score over the end line.

After you feel comfortable with this drill, take some time to practise the dummy pass. Surprise is important for the dummy pass to be successful, so on the occasions the defender holds back to anticipate a pass, you'll need to switch from an intended to a dummy pass. Do not worry if the defender is not fooled by your dummy pass. Having the confidence to try it is what's important.

 **Success Goal** =

a. 10 consecutive successful passes and scores on alternate sides with no forward passes ____
b. 3 successful dummy passes and scores—do not try to dummy each time ____

Success Check

- Take defender away from direction of pass ____
- Pass when defender is committed to tackling ____
- Both hands on ball to pass ____
- Find support runner ____
- Focus on defender and support runner ____

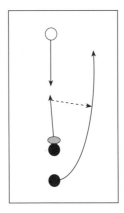

To Increase Difficulty

- Run at about 75 percent of full speed.
- Start with ball on the ground, run in and pick it up as you attack the defence.
- Shorten the space between you and defender.
- Support runner must start outside work area, in a different place each time.

To Decrease Difficulty

- Defender must follow the first ball carrier, not the pass or the receiver.
- The defender may only walk.

4. 3 vs. 2 Grid Drill

Succeeding with a 3 vs. 2 passing situation is a very difficult task unless you are generally successful with the 2 vs. 1 situation. To be successful with the 3 vs. 2, you must fix the first defender and hold off the pass long enough to put the next, or link, ball handler under pressure. The link player has to catch then pass in one movement to avoid being tackled. In a successful 3 vs. 2 situation, this sequence of movement is executed so close to the defenders as to make it impossible for either of them to drift across from one attacker to the next.

You must also angle your running lines to drag both defenders away from the area you and your partners wish to attack. The person you pass to must be able to give and take a pass in one running stride, otherwise the defenders will be able to move across and tackle the outside running player before the goal line can be threatened.

Give yourself plenty of width to begin with—20 metres will be sufficient—and play over a distance of about 15 metres. The defenders should stand on the far goal line 2 metres apart and should move forward as the practice begins. The first defender must be responsible for the ball carrier. The other defender is free to defend against either of the other two attackers.

If you are the ball carrier, you will take the first defender toward the nearest touch line to create space for the next two attackers. Once you see that the defender is fully committed to that running line, turn to look at the support and make ready to pass.

If you are a support runner, run 2 metres behind the ball carrier. This will give you time to pass the ball on should it come to your target. If you also angle your running line to copy that of the first ball carrier, you will create space for the third player and take the defender away from where you intend to pass.

Defenders will often approach at different speeds and from various angles, so you must practise for such situations. Always practise at match pace so that you prepare for the game realistically. After you have mastered the original grid, widen the space in which you work.

Mastering simple practices such as these helps you to become more successful in the game. You should try to misshape the defence to create a situation in which an attacker can run at a gap in the defence. Sometimes this gap is between two of the players and at other times it will be around the outside edge. In the full game, this situation most often occurs when the centres and full back have managed to confine the defence into a narrow space and give the winger a clear run down the touch line. Many of the game's best tries have been scored in this way.

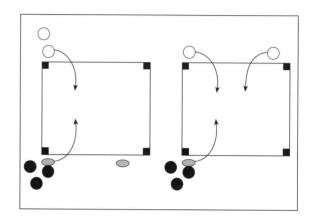

Success Goal = 5 consecutive successful attempts at scoring ___

Success Check
• Make a target for the pass ___
• Stay behind ball carrier until ball is about to be passed ___
• Accelerate to the ball ___
• Choose running line that creates space for others ___
• Pass only when defender is committed ___

To Increase Difficulty
• Work at game intensity in the grid.
• Shorten the distance between ball carrier and defenders.
• Support runners start from different points along the side of work area.
• Start by rolling the ball into the area. This is the trigger for everyone to move.
• Narrow the work area.

To Decrease Difficulty
• Defenders are to follow only their designated attacker.
• Defenders may only walk, attackers may run.

5. Switch Passing Down a Channel

This drill provides pair practice of the switch pass and introduces variable defensive pressure.

a. Mark out a channel to run down. Space the markers evenly down the edge of both sides of the channel. After making a switch pass at the centre of the channel, run outside the next pair of markers and across the centre again for another switch pass. You should practise this drill until you make no mistakes with any of the passes as either receiver or passer. Remember that the receiver should take the ball at chest height so that he or she does not have to look down when catching it.

b. Practise the timing of the pass against a defender. Although this is not a realistic position from the defence's point of view, start by allowing the defender to stand at the centre of the grid. Once you become used to playing close to the defender, you can allow the defender to move and also touch tackle the ball carrier.

The skill is to make the defender touch tackle the wrong person, that is, not the ball carrier. You can do this only if you introduce the dummy switch into the game. As the practice develops, the ball carrier and the support player can begin to alter the angles at which they run, and they can stay within the channel rather than going outside the marker cones.

Sometimes the run can be shallow, at other times much more angled to the other player. The defender too can alter positions, so that all three players become used to putting the opposition at a disadvantage.

You may have as many defenders in the channel as you wish, but there must be at least 10 metres from one to the next so that you can practise running at the correct angles for making a switch pass. Defenders should change their starting positions so that you can practise working at different angles.

c. Another variation of the drill is called five lives—five attempts at scoring against three defenders with 15 metres between defenders. As the attack develops, try to work in a switch pass. Defenders may move only sideways.

Success Goals =

a. No mistakes in passing or catching, moving as fast as possible one channel length and back ____
b. Up channel and back, maintaining momentum, without a defender touch tackling ball carrier ____
c. 5 successful attempts at scoring ____

Success Check

- Keep ball visible to receiver ____
- Lob ball gently in front of receiver's hands ____
- Turn head and upper body to look at target ____
- Signal when you want receiver to cross behind ____
- Receiver makes target and accelerates to the ball ____

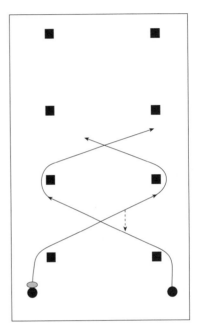

To Increase Difficulty

Drills a and b:
- Alter the angles of your running lines so that they do not match, sometimes parallel to the side of the channel.
- Change running speed so that the receiver is running flat out as the pass is delivered. You will have to practise the correct timing sequence for the safe delivery of the pass.
- Defenders try to touch the ball carrier; introduce the dummy switch to confuse the defenders.
- Defenders may move from side to side.

Drill c:
- Allow defenders to move forward as soon as the one in front is beaten.
- Roll the ball into the grid, chase it, pick it up and begin play.
- Let the defender throw the ball up in the air for you to retrieve and then attack.
- Make your game channel narrower.

To Decrease Difficulty

Drills a and b:
- Place a marker at the centre of the channel in each square, and make your passes directly over the top of the marker.
- Run quickly but never at full speed to control the movement of the ball.
- Pass early with a little more height.
- Passer and receiver talk to each other to coordinate passing and catching.
- Defender may not knock the ball down, but must say if the ball was visible to the defence at the point of release.

Drill c:
- Allow more space between defenders.

6. Loop Pass Drill

Practise loop passing in pairs and then threes without opposition. Work down a 15-metre-wide channel and continuously loop around the ball carrier. As ball carrier, you must always angle your run slightly away from the direction of the next pass, so that you create space at your side for the next player to run into. Pass into the space with sufficient power for the ball to go no higher than the receiver's shoulder. Pass only when you have seen the receiver move into the space to your side. If you are the receiver, you should accelerate to the ball and through the gap in front of you.

After you have achieved the success goal without defence, add three defenders to practise attacking the gap between two of them. Make sure that you run hard toward the defence. In a real game this makes defenders focus their attention on the ball carrier and not on the looping player. As first ball carrier, you must attract the defence. Once you have fixed the first defender, you can then pass and loop. If the second ball carrier runs slightly back and across, you will find it easy to loop round. If not, you may find yourself running slightly back toward your own goal line in order to hit the gap. The ball carrier should then accelerate hard to make it easier for you to head downfield as you receive the pass in the gap.

Success Goal = 10 successful loop passes with no mistakes ___

Success Check
- Runner hits gap at pace parallel to touch lines ___
- Pass at shoulder height into gap ___
- Create space for pass ___
- Do not pass until receiver has started to run ___
- Move onto running line before receiving pass and accelerate hard ___

To Increase Difficulty
- Catch and pass in one stride to the looping player. You can do this only if you are committed to a running line back toward the looping player.
- Assume the receiver will get there! Pass without looking.
- Bring the defenders a little closer to shorten time to make the pass.
- Work at match pace.
- Complete a sequence of lateral passing once the loop pass has been made.
- Include a fourth defender as a full back and to score.

To Decrease Difficulty
- Hold the ball for a few strides before passing, but be sure that the receiver does not run ahead of you before you can make the pass.
- Talk your way through the passing sequence so that the receiver knows when you will pass.
- Defenders play one-on-one defence so that gaps occur.

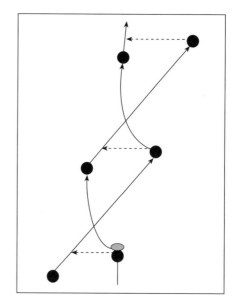

7. Playing Against Active Defence

In this drill the defence will be allowed to drift across from one attacker to the next. You will now find that fixing your opponent is very important. At times you may need to use a dummy pass to create a gap for another player or yourself. On the practice ground do not be afraid to attempt any kind of manoeuvre. This is the only way that you will learn and improve.

Set up your defence at different angles and also alter the shape of the attacking line. Sometimes begin flat with the players close together, at other times begin deep or with a combination (first two players deep from the first passer and others much flatter). See which gives you the most options for attack. It is not where you are when you start to run that is important; rather, it is where you are when the ball is passed—too flat and you may overrun the pass, too deep and you may collect the passer's tackler as well as your own.

In this practice you should try to attack the spaces that are already there. Sometimes you may have to widen them by running at an angle. Then by making a loop pass or a miss (skip) or a dummy loop, continue the attack by passing to other players who are in better positions to either penetrate or overlap the defence.

Success Goal = 3 out of 5 successful scoring attempts, always crossing tackle line of defence ____

Success Check
- Float pass slightly into gap for accuracy ____
- Pass upward so ball is taken at shoulder height ____
- Check running lines to hold defence ____

To Increase Difficulty
- Allow defence to organise their defensive system.
- Allow defenders free movement to tackle any attacker.

To Decrease Difficulty
- Defenders must play one-on-one defence.
- Restrict the movement of each individual defender.

8. Passing Sequences

The purpose of this drill is to link a range of action sequences together to practise attacking a multi-layered defence. Throughout the game of rugby, recurring situations sometimes require improvisation, at other times, a structured attack. Good players recognise such needs immediately and respond accordingly. This drill puts you in such fluid attacking situations and demands a range of decisions from you. You may need to use a lateral pass to penetrate or outflank the defence, or a switch or loop to create space, or you may need to improvise a pass to meet the need of the attack. If it works, it is correct!

Use a channel approximately 22 metres wide and 50 metres long. Place two or three pairs of defenders at random in the channel. As you become more proficient, you can add more single defenders to the opposition. Initially, you may restrict the defenders to moving only sideways, but eventually they should be allowed to defend their goal line as they wish.

Success Goal = 5 scores from 5 attempts ____

Success Check
- Misshape defence each time you go for a score ____
- Attack approaching defence—use your eyes! ____
- Pull defenders from where they want to be into positions of disadvantage ____

To Increase Difficulty
- Gradually make each layer of the defence active.
- Allow any defender who has been passed to follow the attack from behind to try to stop the momentum of the ball carrier.

To Decrease Difficulty
- Defenders may defend only their zone.
- Defenders defend an individual attacker, leaving other players free to run.

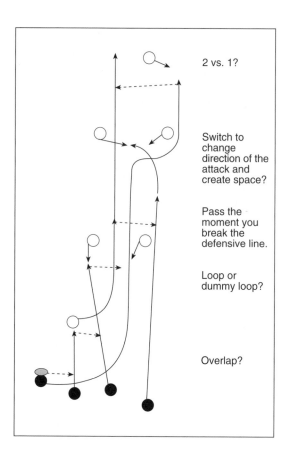

2 vs. 1?

Switch to change direction of the attack and create space?

Pass the moment you break the defensive line.

Loop or dummy loop?

Overlap?

PASSING AND RECEIVING SUCCESS SUMMARY

You may be a naturally gifted player who does not need the structure of a drill to develop your skills. You might prefer to learn by playing modified rugby games and return to the practice drills only when you need to learn a handling technique in a controlled and structured environment. Have a coach or teammate check your technique against the Keys to Success earlier in this chapter. Remember that you should not alter your passing style if it is successful in delivering a wide variety of passes with sufficient accuracy to allow the receiver a range of options.

On the other hand you may be new to the game and will need to use the practice drills in order to build on your ability to play. For those just starting out it is essential to realise that you must always carry the ball so that you can pass it to someone in a better position than yourself. Direction is given by holding the ball in the fingers and pushing towards the catcher with the hands.

As a catcher you can assist the passer by holding your hands at chest height, palms facing the ball carrier as a target. This assists greatly when the ball needs to be passed in close contact situations. As you gain experience you will discover that rugby is a game of running, passing, catching and collision. In order to avoid these collisions with your opponents you will need to master your passing skills.

STEP 3

FOOTWORK: BEATING YOUR OPPONENT

There are many situations in a game that may isolate the ball carrier. It is as much the responsibility of the ball carrier to find support as it is for the support to find the ball carrier, but the reality is that occasionally you cannot help becoming isolated when you're carrying the ball. You often may be isolated when you have been put through a widening gap, and you may have only one player to beat in order to score. At times like these you will have to rely on different ways of beating the last defender.

Pure speed is probably the best and easiest way of beating a defence but sometimes the defender is in a position that makes it difficult for you to use speed alone. Also, you won't always be as fast as your opponent. You therefore need to develop some of your natural dodging skills.

Besides pure speed, basic evasive skills consist of changing pace, swerving, and sidestepping. The ability to run at speed while moving on and off a straight line makes it very difficult for any tackler to line you up for a decisive tackle. This type of running is difficult to develop if you do not have basic agility. If you play a number of sports it is highly likely that this will begin to develop quite naturally while practising and playing. If not, you might now consider playing another sport such as basketball or work with a group of friends to develop a series of running practices which encourage changes of speed and direction. You can also play tag and dodge games with the group and these will also develop your evasive running skills.

A player who can beat a defender by speed or agility or a combination of both is an asset to any team. Such players break out of their own 22-metre area to set up an attack or take on the last defender and still score or breach even the tightest of defences to create opportunities for others. To help you get the most from your running ability, and to select the best options for a given situation, this chapter introduces you to the basic evasive skills of changing pace, the sidestep and the swerve and offers drills to help you to develop these running techniques.

Each player in the team should have evasive-skill practice to make the unit more efficient. As with all your other practice, it is best to start with a passive defence to become used to the pressure that a defender exerts. Make sure that you dominate the defender at all times. The defender should react to you, not the other way round. At times when a defender has already closed off certain areas of attack, however, you must attack the defence so that you re-establish your advantage as ball carrier.

Increasing Running Speed

Most athletic clubs have a specialist coach for sprinters. If you wish to increase your running speed, you should consult your nearest specialist coach for advice; however, initially you can begin by increasing the speed of your leg movements (cadence) and the length of your stride. You can increase stride length by improving the flexibility of your leg joints and by increasing the length and suppleness of your leg muscles, especially the hamstrings. Leg speed will improve only if you use a range of exercises specifically designed to work on your knee lift, stride, speed of contact and lift from the ground. As you mature, you will also begin to develop power in your running with constant practice and specific strength work to develop running force.

Evading a Defender Using a Change of Pace

When you are ball carrier, tacklers calculate where the tackle will occur by judging your speed and direction and set off to intercept your running line (see diagram 3.1). When faced by a tackler, you have a range of decisions to make that depend on the tackler's angle of approach and the space available for you to evade him or her. If there is little space on the outside and the inside gap is covered, your lateral movement options are limited; it is likely that you will need to pull the defender toward you by using a change of pace as a ploy and then accelerate away (see diagram 3.2).

You begin this strategy by first slowing down slightly. This will force the defender to change direction slightly and choose a new line for the tackle. Once the defender commits to this new angle of approach, you accelerate away. Your change of pace manoeuvre may also include a slight swerve away from the direction of the would-be tackler. All players should try to perfect this evasive skill because it puts a tackler at a disadvantage and allows the ball carrier to stretch the defence.

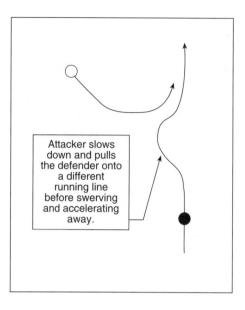

Attacker slows down and pulls the defender onto a different running line before swerving and accelerating away.

Diagram 3.2 Change your pass and accelerate away.

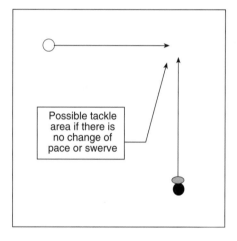

Possible tackle area if there is no change of pace or swerve

Diagram 3.1 Tacklers run to intercept your running line.

How to Execute the Sidestep

When running toward an opponent at an angle, sometimes you will wish to quickly change the direction of the attack. To do this you trick the defender by running in one direction and then quickly stepping off one foot to head off at a different angle. This move is called a sidestep. Many young players can do this quite naturally, especially if they play other team sports in which they have to dodge and weave.

To perform a sidestep well, you need to understand the basics. First, you must decide where you next wish to attack and then begin to angle away from that area. As the defender begins to close in on you, accelerate, then step wide with the outside leg at the same time leaning your body weight directly over the top of that foot (see figure 3.1a). This will suggest to the defender that you are trying to attack the outside space. As the defender also moves outward, drive off the outside leg back inside, thus "wrong-footing" the defence (see figure 3.1b).

FIGURE
3.1 **KEYS TO SUCCESS**

SIDESTEP

a   b   c

Preparation	**Execution**	**Follow-Through**
1. Choose running angle to take defender away from chosen attacking line ___ 2. Ball in two hands ___	1. Plant outside foot, shifting weight over that foot ___ 2. Shift weight quickly away from planted foot and drive past defender to the inside ___ 3. Watch defender constantly ___	1. Accelerate into open space ___ 2. Look for support or the goal line ___

Sidesteps are easy to learn but difficult to execute, especially against a defender. Usually the quick change of direction causes the most difficulty for attackers. A simple way to experience the feel of a sidestep is to step onto a slope and use the incline to push against (see figure 3.2). As you become better at the skill, you decrease the slope until you can perform the sidestep well on a flat surface.

How to Execute the Swerve

The swerve is sometimes used when you have committed yourself to a running line and the defender is very close to making a tackle on you. In this situation you draw the defender in close (see figure 3.3a) and then alter your running line to take your legs away from the defender's outstretched arms (see figure 3.3b). If you are swerving to the left, run on the

Figure 3.2 Step onto a slope.

inside edge of your left boot and the outside edge of your right as you travel past the defender. When you swerve left, hold the ball with your left hand and arm and pull it in to the left side of your chest. Use the opposite side when swerving to the right. At the same time, try to lean toward the defender with your shoulders, and if it is allowed in your game, fend off the defender with your arm and hand.

Sometimes you may receive a pass when there's space between you and the defender. When this happens, threaten the space behind the defender and then lean and swerve away, accelerating as hard as you can. If you can also add a controlled change of pace into your swerve, you will be very difficult to tackle.

FIGURE 3.3

KEYS TO SUCCESS

SWERVE

a   b   c

Preparation

1. Run toward defender's inside shoulder ___
2. Hold ball either to the ribs or in two hands ___
3. Control your pace ___

Execution

1. As defender moves toward you, accelerate away hard ___
2. Use edges of feet to help you lean away and swerve ___
3. Watch defender constantly ___

Follow-Through

1. Run into space, toward goal line ___
2. Look for support ___

FOOTWORK SUCCESS STOPPERS

Error	Correction
1. You find it difficult to change speed when running.	1. You are probably running too quickly to begin with and so you have little control. Slow down at the start and you will be able to change speed and direction more easily.
2. Your sidestep is ineffective against a defender.	2. You are probably approaching the defender directly head on. You should run at an angle, away from your intended attack area. As soon as the defender is committed to your running line, change direction immediately.
3. You find it difficult to change direction with your sidestep.	3. You should practise driving your foot hard into a slope to develop your change of direction. At the same time allow your body weight to move over the foot on the slope. This persuades your opponent that you intend to continue running in that direction. You then drive off into the space behind the nearest defender.
4. Even though you have a good swerve, you are easily caught by the defender.	4. Either you are running too close to the defender before you swerve, or your running line is too shallow. Try to run first at the space behind the defender before you accelerate and change direction.
5. You can swerve through only the first few gaps in a line of markers before you miss a gap.	5. Run a little slower so that you keep your balance. Lean over the top of the marker and dig the edges of your boots hard into the playing surface.
6. You always seem to be caught by the defender when you have a decision to make.	6. Your priority is to run at the space away from where you intend to attack. Leave plenty of space between you and any defender; slow down if necessary. As soon as the defender slows or is committed to a change of direction, make your move as fast as possible.

FOOTWORK

DRILLS

1. Speed Up/Slow Down

Before you try to beat a defender, you should become used to the feeling of accelerating hard from a running start. To accelerate, increase your stride length and leg speed. Practise accelerating from different speeds, for example, from jogging to three-quarters speed, from three-quarters to full pace. As you accelerate hard, swerve to the left or the right. Try to reach your target speed as quickly as possible. A smooth, slow build-up of speed allows the defender to speed up as well. Surprise is everything.

Although a change of pace may occur on a long run in for a try, the actual change of pace covers only a few metres, so you should practise over relatively short distances of approximately 20 metres. When you try the change of pace, it is a good idea to set out a range of markers to follow so that your running line and acceleration distance are clearly visible when running.

Success Goal = 5 times through markers without slipping or touching a marker ___

✔ **Success Check**
• Accelerate smoothly and quickly ___
• Change pace quickly ___
• Watch defender constantly ___

To Increase Difficulty
• Make swerve more pronounced by moving markers outward.
• Work at three-quarters to full pace.

To Decrease Difficulty
• Practise down a straight line.
• Work slowly until you've mastered different speeds.

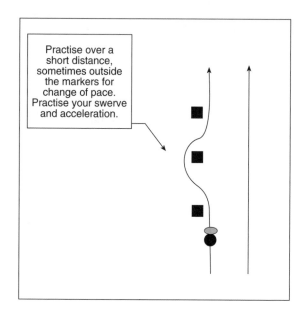

Practise over a short distance, sometimes outside the markers for change of pace. Practise your swerve and acceleration.

2. Defender Chase

To practise your change of pace, always have the defender approach from one side and slightly behind so that you find it impossible to sidestep. It is up to you to draw the defender in close by slowing your run and then accelerating hard away and slightly outward (provided there is room between you and the touch line).

a. For this part of the drill, place your markers from the 10m line to goal line so that the defender will approach from behind you as you enter the 22m area. The defender must wait for you as ball carrier to start your run. After starting your run, you must move into the 22-metre area quickly so that you can attract the attention of the defender. As soon as you can, slow slightly to pull the defender toward you, then accelerate hard and swerve away to score at the goal line.

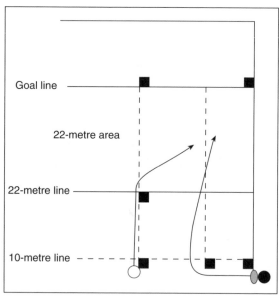

Goal line

22-metre area

22-metre line

10-metre line

b. In this part of the drill, you practise scoring as well as evasion. Use the lines marked on the field to gauge where the markers should be placed. Always mark the goal line at the end of the channel. Set the defender's markers slightly behind those for the attacker. Your intention is to win the race for the score at the corner marker. If the defender's markers are too far to the side, you will score too easily; too far in and you will never beat the defender. Choose a defender who is about your speed or slightly faster—this is the only way to improve. Place the markers by gauging the speeds of each player and altering the distances accordingly.

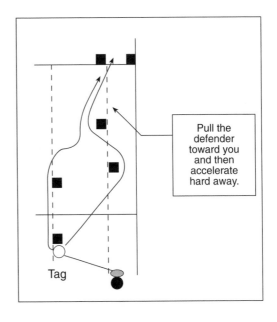

Pull the defender toward you and then accelerate hard away.

Tag

Each time you start your run, aim toward the defender, make a touch tackle and then sprint away and around the marker toward the goal line. The chaser will be close to you as you round the first marker, so you should keep looking to decide when to accelerate hard: too late and you will be caught, too early and you may slide as you round the marker.

Success Goal = 7 successful evasions out of 10 tries ____

Success Check
- Control your speed ____
- If you have space, beat defender by speed alone ____
- Pull defender close, then accelerate and swerve away ____
- Watch defender constantly ____

To Increase Difficulty
- Move goal line closer to defender.
- Move defender's and ball carrier's markers closer together.

To Decrease Difficulty
- Widen goal line on ball carrier's side.
- Move defender's and ball carrier's markers farther apart.

3. Slalom Course

Organise a slalom course using as many corner flags or markers as you can find (see diagram a). Set up each set of gates so that you have to change direction to go from one gate to the next. The more gates you have, the more you can practise your agility running and the quicker you may improve.

To feel the rhythm required to swerve through these obstacles, begin by walking and gradually increase your pace. It is almost impossible to work at maximum speed, so you must control your speed through the gates. Except when racing side by side with an opponent for the goal line, you must control your running speed to take best advantage of your opportunities when trying to beat a defender in a game.

You should now be ready to practise at match pace. This is not necessarily running as fast as you can. You should run so that you are still in control of your body weight and can dodge and weave. The faster you can do this under control, the better.

Success Goal = Fast movement through all gates without touching any ___

Success Check

• Run at controlled speed ___
• Look ahead and plan which gates to go through next ___

To Increase Difficulty

• Put a team of players at the opposite end of the slalom course working in the opposite direction so that you have to pass one of their players (b).
• Use a number of teams at each end of the slalom course so that you must avoid players working in the same and in the opposite direction (b).

To Decrease Difficulty

• Widen the spaces between the gates.

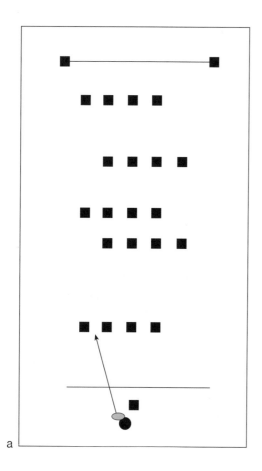

4. Sidestepping a Single Defender

Work against a defender in a 10 metre by 10 metre square. You both start at the same time but from different corners along the same edge of the square. As you approach the defender, head toward one corner, then drive your outside leg hard into the ground and drive back inside at the gap. Lower your body weight as you do this in case you have to drive through an outstretched arm. Score on the goal line.

 **Success Goal** = 7 scores out of 10 attempts without contact ___

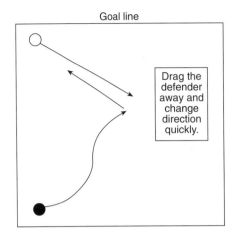

Goal line

Drag the defender away and change direction quickly.

✔ **Success Check**
- Run at pace with control ___
- Drag the defender quickly sideways ___
- As the defender overtakes you slightly, side-step ___
- Vary your attack: If the defender is expecting a sidestep, attack using speed ___

To Increase Difficulty
- Defender starts closer to attacker.
- Narrow the channel.

To Decrease Difficulty
- Defender starts farther away from attacker.

5. Avoiding a Slap

You need to be able to swerve to both sides. Practise against a line of other players who each hold out an alternate arm with a clenched fist: Practise swerving first to one and then to the other side. In this practice you should try to lean toward the "tackler" as far as you can, but keep your body away from the fist. Shift the ball from one side of your body to the other so that it is always at the side farthest from a tackler.

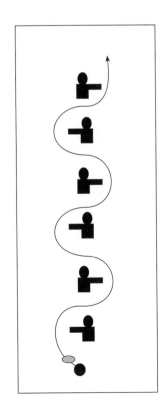

Success Goals =
  a. 5 times up and down line at top speed ___
  b. Complete runs without being slapped on 7 out of 10 ___

✔ **Success Check**
- Run at pace with control ___
- Stay close to fists without touching them ___
- Use outside and inside edges of boots to increase grip ___
- Keep ball away from tacklers ___

To Increase Difficulty
- Allow defenders to try to slap runner's thigh with an open hand.
- Move tacklers closer together.

To Decrease Difficulty
- Increase the distance between tacklers.

6. Combining Moves

Set out a row of markers for attacker and defender along a channel at uneven intervals. You should set out the defender's markers so that the defender approaches from different angles depending on which marker is rounded. The defender decides which marker to run around. You must react to the defence that comes at you. If the defender comes from behind, use speed; if the defender comes directly from the side, consider using your swerve; if the defender comes from straight ahead, use your sidestep.

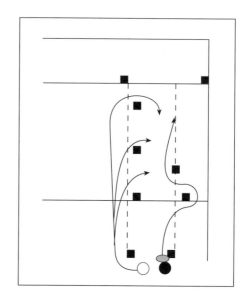

Success Goal = 5 successful runs down the channel ___

Success Check
• Watch defender at all times ___
• Allow defender to come close only in a narrow channel ___
• Always dominate defender ___
• Drag defender away from intended attack area ___

To Increase Difficulty
• Introduce the full tackle when your coach thinks you are ready.
• Narrow the channel.

To Decrease Difficulty
• Specify which marker the defender will run round.
• Widen the channel.
• Move the defender's markers farther from your intended running line.
• Widen the goal line.

FOOTWORK SUCCESS SUMMARY

You may already possess the agility vital to rugby, or you can develop this agility by constant practice against a defence that gradually exerts more and more pressure on you. You can use this agility as part of the way you beat the defence. Although most footwork skills are done while running quickly, they are most easily performed when running at a speed at which you can control your balance. Focus on timing, on keeping under control and on making strong moves to evade your defender. Have a coach or another player check your Keys to Success fundamentals illustrated in figures 3.1 and 3.2.

STEP
4 TACKLING: ATTACK WITHOUT POSSESSION

Winning teams spend at least 50 percent of their time practising defensive techniques and systems to prevent the opposition from scoring. This is because rugby is often 50 percent defence, and good tackling helps to win games. If all members of your team improve their tackling technique, you will increase the amount of pressure you put on the opposition and force them to make mistakes, which will create more opportunities for you to regain control of the ball and therefore control of the game.

If you and your teammates never miss a tackle, the opposition will find it very difficult to score against you. You will severely test their ability to create space in 2 vs. 1 situations. When you make your first-time tackles, you will prevent your opponents from going forward toward your goal line and force them back toward their own goal line. Your well-timed tackles could stop your opponent from passing the ball, making defence easier for the rest of your team. Your pressure tackling could force the opposition to knock-on, or make a forward pass, giving you the advantage of the put-in at the subsequent scrum and controlled possession from which to launch your next attack. You may also gain an advantage by immediately regaining possession of the ball from your opponents' mistake, in which case the referee will often allow you to play on and make progress by attacking what is usually a disorganised defence. You should regard defence as attack without possession.

In this chapter you will learn how to tackle opponents from different positions—from the side, behind and directly in front—because the opposition will attack you from different angles. You often may have to chase back to tackle a player as well. The various tackling techniques and practices in this chapter are carefully structured to maximise your confidence and tackling ability and therefore your contribution and efficiency in game situations. Each practice is designed to gradually lead you up the staircase to tackling success.

The best way to practise tackling against a partner is from a kneeling position and then to gradually progress to walking, jogging and finally full-paced tackling. It is a good idea to take your boots or trainers off for your first tackling session, which should be on soft ground or spongy gym mats. Make sure that you practise with someone about your own size and weight and that you are thoroughly warmed up before you start your tackling practice. Use some non-competitive strengthening exercises, like piggy-back walks, and bear hug lifts and walks over a 5- or 10-metre distance, to prepare for your contact practice. When tackling, never attempt to trip up your opponent with your feet: Tripping is dangerous and illegal. You also are not allowed to tackle around the neck or above shoulder height because it is very dangerous.

As part of tackling practice, it is also important for you to practise making contact with the ground safely when you fall. Although this will be dealt with in more detail in Step 6, be aware of safe falling practices as you take your tackling up to speed. When being tackled, go with the flow of the impact because this will help you to land and roll naturally. You should round your shoulder as you prepare to hit the ground and land mainly on your back and side. Tuck your chin into your chest as you land. Bend your knees, keeping them tucked up, and resist the urge to put a straight arm or hand out to break your fall because you may injure yourself. After you execute a tackle, always get back on your feet as quickly as possible to rejoin the game.

Rugby union rules state that when a ball carrier is tackled, he or she must pass or release the ball immediately, move away from the ball and get up on his or her feet before playing the ball again. If the ball carrier falls down with the ball without being held, he or she can get up and continue running forward. When you tackle the ball carrier, grip your opponent tightly as you both land on the ground to ensure that the player has to release the ball.

Once you become a skilled tackler and seasoned rugby player, you will find that executing a good tackle can be as satisfying as scoring a good try.

How to Execute the Side Tackle

Start your practice of the side tackle from a kneeling position. As the ball carrier approaches, prepare for the tackle by keeping your head up, chin off your chest, and your back flat. With your shoulders braced for impact, seek to place your head behind the ball carrier's legs, going "cheek to cheek" (see figure 4.1a). The best contact is made in the dip where your shoulder meets your neck. Wrap your hands around the player's legs, and drive up and through with your legs, keeping your eyes open and holding on tightly. Try to fall on top of the attacker (see figure 4.1b).

FIGURE 4.1

KEYS TO SUCCESS

SIDE TACKLE

a

b

c

Preparation

1. Watch ball carrier ___
2. Keep head up, chin off chest, back flat ___
3. Look forward ___
4. Head behind the ball carrier's legs "cheek to cheek" ___

Execution

1. Shoulder braced, contact on thigh ___
2. Wrap arms around thighs, pull and hold tight ___
3. Don't intertwine fingers ___
4. Keep eyes open ___
5. Drive up and through ball carrier with legs ___

Follow-Through

1. Hold tight ___
2. Turn ball carrier sideways ___
3. Try to land on top of ball carrier ___

How to Execute the Front Tackle

In the front tackle you use your opponent's forward momentum to your advantage to bring him or her down. Don't try to drive the attacker backward until you are a lot more experienced and stronger. Start the front tackle from a kneeling position or squat position, then progress to a crouching or standing start.

As the ball carrier approaches, look up into his or her legs and ribs and move your head and neck to one side of the ball carrier's body (see figure 4.2a). Shrug your shoulders on contact and drive your shoulder into the attacker's ribcage as you wrap your arms around his or her thighs. Using the ball carrier's momentum, sit and fall backward as you turn (see figure 4.2b). This will allow you to bring the attacker over your shoulder as you fall on top (see figure 4.2c).

FIGURE 4.2 **KEYS TO SUCCESS**

FRONT TACKLE

Preparation

1. Watch ball carrier ____
2. Look up into thighs and ribs ____
3. Keep back flat ____
4. Move head and neck to one side of ball carrier's body, "cheek to cheek" ____

Execution

1. Shrug shoulders on contact ____
2. Drive shoulder up into lower ribs ____
3. Wrap arms around ball carrier's thighs and hold tight ____
4. Follow ball carrier's momentum: Sit, fall backward and turn ____

Follow-Through

1. Allow player to fall over your shoulder ____
2. Turn ball carrier sideways and land on top ____

How to Execute the Rear Tackle

Sometimes you need to turn and run up behind to catch and tackle an opponent to stop him or her from scoring or gaining ground. To do this at pace, you need to time your tackle carefully to be sure you make solid contact. Remember to wear training shoes or bare feet when you first try this type of tackle.

To execute the rear tackle, try to place your head behind or to the side of the ball carrier's buttocks as you grip tightly around his or her thighs and drive forward with your shoulder (see figure 4.3). Pull the ball carrier's legs inward and try to fall on top of the attacker. Sometimes, especially near your own line, a smother tackle is useful, in which you wrap your arms around your opponent's arms and the ball, preventing a pass to support players.

FIGURE 4.3 **KEYS TO SUCCESS**

REAR TACKLE

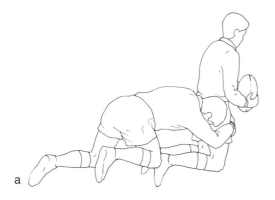

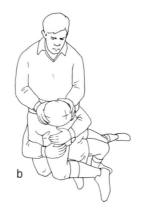

Preparation	Execution	Follow-Through
1. Watch player, time your contact ___ 2. Head up, back flat ___ 3. Head and neck behind player's buttocks or to side ___	1. Shoulder into buttocks ___ 2. Arms around thighs, squeeze tight ___ 3. Drive forward with shoulder ___	1. Pull ball carrier's legs to side ___ 2. Land on top ___

TACKLING SUCCESS STOPPERS

Getting comfortable with tackling a ball carrier from any angle takes practice. Start from a static tackling position and progress to walking, jogging and then full movement. For more effective tackling, rather than waiting for the attacking player to control your movements, move toward the attacker, keeping infield, and force them toward the touch line before you pounce. Never attempt to trip up your opponents or tackle them around the neck or above shoulder height: It is illegal and dangerous. To make sure you tackle safely, correct your errors. Here are some tips and correct technique reminders:

Error	Correction
1. You tackle with your head down and eyes closed.	1. Keep your head up and use your eyes to aim for the point of contact, usually around the thigh region.
2. You tackle with your fingertips and are brushed aside.	2. Aim to make contact with your shoulder at a point at least 1 metre beyond the attacker. Get into low, effective driving position. Hold on tightly, even when you first fall on the ground.
3. Your tackle is unsuccessful because you put your head in front of opponent's legs.	3. Remember: "cheek to cheek", head and face behind opponent's buttocks.
4. You forget to drive off the ground with your feet and legs.	4. Bend your knees and lower your hips as you explode, and spring off the balls of your feet. Make shoulder contact first.
5. You are caught on your heels out of position.	5. Try to move forward toward the attacker. Shepherd the attacker into a space you can control, often toward the touch line, leaving the attacker only one direction to move in.

TACKLING

DRILLS

1. Side-Tackle Progression

In this basic tackling drill, you work in a small (8 metre by 8 metre) grid area. Begin tackling on your knees, and progress to standing, running tackles.

a. Kneel down next to your partner. Tackler gets into the starting position to make a static side tackle. Remember to practise "cheek to cheek" and to grab your opponent around the thighs. After reaching your success goal, have your partner stand and move forward while you remain on your knees.
b. Tackler stands and crouches as the attacker walks forward and is tackled from the side. Remember to keep your head up, drive your shoulder into your opponent's thigh and hold on tight. Progress from a walk, to a jog and finally to a run each time you achieve your success goal.

Success Goal = 3 successful tackles each with right and left shoulders ___

✔ Success Check

- Keep eyes open and look at target ___
- Head behind legs and seat, "cheek to cheek" ___
- Make contact with shoulder on thigh ___
- Hold on tight ___
- Drive with legs ___

To Increase Difficulty

- (a) Your partner moves forward on his or her knees. You try to side tackle before your partner gets past you and scores on the opposite side of the grid.
- (b) Starting on the end line, your partner carries a ball and tries to get past you to score. After each try by your opponent, you must touch the opposite side line before your next tackle attempt. How many tries can your partner score in 30 seconds?

To Decrease Difficulty

- Start on your knees, or go back to having your opponent walk, and use the shoulder you feel most comfortable tackling with.

2. Front-Tackle Progression

Work in an 8 metre by 8 metre grid area. Face your partner and crouch down to prepare to make a front tackle. Your opponent walks alternately to your left then right shoulder. Remember to use your opponent's forward momentum to your advantage when tackling: Sit, fall backward and turn to execute the tackle. After reaching your success goal, change places with your partner.

Success Goal = 3 successful tackles each with right and left shoulders ___

✔ Success Check

- Move head to side of opponent's body ___
- Hold on tight ___
- Use opponent's momentum and weight to your advantage ___
- Turn opponent, and land on top ___

To Increase Difficulty

- Have your opponent try to jog then run past you.
- Roll a ball to your partner who picks it up and attempts to jog past you and score on the goal line. Your partner can choose on which side to try to pass to you to keep you guessing. If your partner scores, he or she should turn around immediately and attempt to score on the other goal line. Trade with your partner after 3 tackles, then move up to running.
- See how many tackles you can make in 10 seconds.

To Decrease Difficulty

- Ask your partner to walk toward the shoulder you feel most comfortable tackling with.

3. Rear-Tackle Progression

Work in an 8 metre by 8 metre grid area. Kneel down slightly behind your partner, both facing the same direction. Get into a comfortable starting position to make a rear tackle (see figure 4.3). After reaching your success goal, try this variation: Say "go" and have your partner try to move forward as quickly as possible on his or her knees to avoid your diving tackle. Don't forget to hold on tightly.

Success Goal = 3 successful tackles each with right and left shoulders ____

Success Check

- Keep eyes open and look at target (upper thighs) ____
- Head and neck to opponent's side—"cheek to cheek" ____
- Shoulder into buttocks, arms around thighs, grip tightly ____
- Land on top ____

To Increase Difficulty

- You and your partner start in a push-up position on all fours next to each other. On your "go", your partner tries to crawl away before you can make the tackle.
- Standing in a crouched position, have your partner walk from behind you carrying a ball. As your partner walks past, dive to tackle. Repeat at a jog, then running.

To Decrease Difficulty

- Use a static kneeling starting position, and tackle with the shoulder you are most comfortable with.

TACKLING SUCCESS SUMMARY

If every player in your team works hard to develop their tackling techniques, you will be a difficult team to beat. Before you start any contact practice it is important to warm up thoroughly. You can do some non-competitive strengthening exercises with a partner about the same size as you. These could include a variety of partner lifts and walks over a 5- or 10-metre distance, for example, piggy-back walks and bear-hug lifts and walks. Ask a friend or teacher to watch your tackling practice and to give you feedback on your technique and progress. If you are determined, you will be successful and have a lot of fun making try-saving tackles. Remember to practise "cheek to cheek": no one can run without legs.

STEP

5

KICKING: ACHIEVING AN ADVANTAGE

G ood, accurate kicking wins games, and poor, aimless kicking loses games. If you learn to kick the ball accurately and with precision, you will make an important contribution to your team. Usually the scrum half, fly half and full back are the players who will do the most kicking. However, every player on your team should be able to kick with some degree of accuracy and skill.

Your teammates also should all be able to catch a ball safely and under control to regain and maintain possession of the ball. If your opponents are accurate kickers, you will be under extreme pressure when trying to catch the ball. Teammates greatly respect—and spectators greatly admire—players who can keep their concentration and secure the ball for their team with a safe catch when there is chaos around them. If you knock the ball forward, you will give away a scrum to the opposition and lose possession of the ball for your team.

While we encourage you to run and pass the ball as much as possible in your games, there may be a crucial moment in the game when your best option is to kick the ball. It may be in your best interest to keep the ball in play and avoid touch (placing the ball out of bounds). So you must make sure you don't aimlessly kick away your possession. Sometimes if you accurately keep the ball in the 5-metre channel area, (5 metres in from the touch line), your opponents have a narrow angle to use when they field the ball and can manage only to kick the ball a short distance into touch. This will give you an opportunity to regain possession by having control of the throw-in at the subsequent line-out. This proves that you need to kick with purpose, rather than as a last resort because you cannot think of anything else to do.

In this chapter, you will learn the most important kicks in rugby union and also how to successfully catch a ball that has been kicked.

Types of Kicks

There are two basic ways of kicking the ball: from your hand (the punt, chip kick, box kick, grubber kick and wipers kick) or from the ground (the place kick and drop kick). Each type of kick plays a distinct and important role for the team with possession.

Kicks From Your Hands

1. There are three types of *punts:*
   a. A high up and under "bomb" that allows chasing players to regain possession behind the defence. For this punt, you need to give the ball enough height to allow time for your chasers to race up field and catch the ball or put pressure on the catcher.
   b. A long touch kick (kicking the ball off the field) for gaining field position or territory.
   c. A long, rolling kick near the touch line to force the opposition to put the ball into touch, so your team has the throw-in at the subsequent line-out. Though similar to a grubber kick, this kick is usually much longer.
2. You use a *chip kick* to kick just over the top of an advancing defence, when you see a space behind the defence. You try to catch your chip kick before the ball hits the ground.
3. If you are playing scrum half, you would *box kick* from the base of the scrum, often on the right-hand side of the field for your right winger and centres to chase and put pressure on the defence. You need to get the ball to hang in the air to buy time for your chasers. (Note: A box kick is similar to a bomb kick, but the technique is notably different.)
4. You can use a *grubber kick* to move the ball along the ground in such a way as to make it

difficult for opponents to control. When you find yourself isolated outside of your 22-metre safety area, you could use this kick to gain territory or to force a line-out. If the defence is coming up quickly, you can direct an angled grubber kick through a gap between the opposition players, and often one of your backs can regain possession. It's also a useful restart kick in wet weather and can lead to the opposition's knocking-on.

5. The *wipers kick* is a diagonal kick behind the defence for your wingers to chase. A fly half will use this kick if the defence is coming up fast, making it difficult for the centres to play, and there is a space out wide behind the defence. A wipers kick often makes it difficult for the defence to turn and get back in time to prevent your movement forward up the playing field.

Kicks From the Ground

1. To start and restart the game, the *place kick* is used. A place kick is also used for penalty and conversion attempts at goal.

2. You can use a *drop kick* to score 3 points in a game. The drop kick is a vital skill for the fly half to master. You aim to drop kick the ball over the crossbar and between the upright posts. A New Zealand number 8 forward scored a spectacular 45-metre drop goal against England in the semi-final of the 1995 World Cup. You will also need to use a drop kick to restart the game from half way and at 22-metre dropouts.

Why Is Kicking Important?

When you kick the ball, you must know why you are doing it and what advantage you hope to achieve over your opponents. Your teammates, such as the chasers who are directly involved, must know when to expect a kick, and all the team should know where the ball should land.

During a game you are likely to kick the ball both in attack and defence. Your grubber, chip or high kicks should help your teammates regain possession behind a defence, having moved the ball across the gain line (so that the ball is in front of all attacking players). You may kick the ball into a space in order to gain ground and take play deep into opposition territory to expose your opposition's defensive weakness and to ease defensive pressure on your backs. For example, a high punt in the air, or bomb, is a good attacking kick that makes it difficult for the opposition to control the ball, and they have to retreat to cover the catcher. If isolated as the last line of defence player deep in your own territory with the opposition bearing down on you, you may decide to simply kick the ball off the field to stop the game to allow time for your team to regroup and start again. Each player has a number of options, as described here.

If you want to play international rugby, it's important that you start practising now to kick accurately using both feet. You should kick with the foot farthest from the opposition. You should also place your kicks to force defenders to use their weakest foot in response, if they choose to kick the ball, having caught it.

Attempt to improve the accuracy, height and distance of your various kicks. Kicking practice is also a good opportunity for your teammates to practise receiving the ball, from the ground or from the air, and to practise chasing kicks in order to regain possession. Except when you are kicking from deep in your own territory, try to keep the ball in play so your team can keep possession, put the opposition under pressure and get used to positioning themselves to receive returned kicks.

How to Execute the Punt

To punt accurately and well, you need to have good balance and timing. First, you must select your target, deciding where you want the ball to land, and point the ball in the direction in which you want to kick. To start the motion, hold the ball at about waist height and at arm's length away from your body. Hold the ball at a 45-degree angle (as shown in figure 5.1a) to the axis of your foot to get maximum contact with your kicking foot. To kick with your right foot, hold the ball underneath with your right hand near you and left hand farthest away at the top and side of the ball. For a left-footed kick, exchange hands, right hand below the left. Your hands create a channel through which you kick.

Place the ball in one controlled movement at waist height, as if you were stacking something on a shelf, then drop it (see figure 5.1b). Point your toes down. Contact the centre of the ball just above your boot laces with your extended ankle and the hard upper bridge of your foot to impart full power (see figure 5.1c). Your non-kicking leg must provide a firm foundation for your accurate kick. As your foot contacts the ball, your leg should accelerate to maximise the force imparted to the ball.

When on the run, slow and steady yourself just before kicking. You will find that control, timing and a natural fluid action often produce better results than attempting to whack the ball out of the grounds.

For proper follow-through, keep your head down and your body over the ball. Try to finish with a high follow-through, with your foot above head height (see figure 5.1d). Your leg should remain straight, and your toes pointed. For a right-footed kick, your left hand should be almost touching your right foot, and your left shoulder should be forward.

FIGURE 5.1 **KEYS TO SUCCESS**

PUNT

a   b   c   d

Preparation

1. Select target ___
2. Keep eyes on ball ___
3. Point ball in direction of kick ___
4. Hold ball at 45-degree angle ___
5. Hold ball at waist height and arm's length ___
6. Right-footed kick: Hold ball in right hand, left hand at top and side of ball. Left-footed kick: Hold ball in left hand, right hand at top and side ___

Execution

1. Point toes down ___
2. Release ball ___
3. Contact centre of ball just above boot laces ___
4. Non-kicking leg provides firm foundation ___
5. Leg accelerates at impact ___
6. Good control, timing and fluid action ___

Follow-Through

1. Head down, body over ball ___
2. High follow-through, foot above head ___
3. Leg straight, toes pointed ___

How to Execute the Bomb Kick

This kick is similar to the punt, but incorporates a special technique that helps the ball hang in the air, allowing time for your chasers to attempt to regain possession and making it difficult for the opposition to catch. It is often aimed at the opposition's goal posts, and the ball rotates end over end. To execute the bomb kick, hold the ball vertically (upright) with one hand on each side and release it, aiming to kick the bottom point of the ball (see figure 5.2)

Figure 5.2 Executing the bomb kick.

How to Execute the Grubber Kick

Lean forward with your head and eyes over the ball while holding the ball upright across its side seams with one hand on each side (see figure 5.3a). Release the ball and make contact with it just before it lands upright on the ground. Point your toes toward the ground, and make contact with your laces while keeping your bent knee slightly ahead of the ball (see figure 5.3b). Make contact with the upper half of the ball. Follow through with a low, straight leg so the ball moves along the ground (see figure 5.3c).

FIGURE
5.3

**FIGURE
5.3** **KEYS TO SUCCESS**

GRUBBER KICK

a   b   c

Preparation

1. Select target ____
2. Keep eyes on ball ____
3. Keep head over ball ____
4. Lean forward ____
5. Steady yourself if running ____
6. Hold ball on each side across side seams ____
7. Hold ball upright ____

Execution

1. Release ball to fall upright ____
2. Make contact just before ball lands ____
3. Point toes down, make contact with laces ____
4. Keep bent knee slightly ahead of ball ____
5. Make contact with upper half of ball ____

Follow-Through

1. Punch ball along ground ____
2. Leg stays low and straight ____

How to Execute a Drop Kick

Hold the ball on each side with your fingers pointing down or forward (see figure 5.4a). Hold the ball out in front of you at waist height, with your elbows bent slightly inward. Keep your eye on the ball, and release it to drop vertically, upright and angled slightly toward you. As the ball lands on the ground, use your instep to connect with the ball on the half-volley, and sweep through to kick the ball into the air (see figure 5.4b). For the follow-through, your kicking foot swings through high, above head height, and your non-kicking leg supports your weight (see figure 5.4c). Remember to keep your eyes on the ball and the point where it initially lands throughout your drop-kicking action.

FIGURE
5.4

KEYS TO SUCCESS

DROP KICK

a b c

Preparation

1. Select target ___
2. Keep eyes on ball ___
3. Hold ball in front at waist height, elbows bent slightly in ___
4. Hold ball along sides, fingers forward or down ___

Execution

1. Keep head down over ball ___
2. Drop ball upright, angled slightly toward you ___
3. As ball lands, instep connects with ball ___

Follow-Through

1. Non-kicking leg bears your weight ___
2. Kicking foot swings above head height ___
3. Eyes on ball, and the point on the ground where it lands ___

How to Execute the Place Kick

Use a place kick for a penalty kick at goal, a conversion attempt after a try has been scored and to start the game. You will find that a kicking tee, a bit like a golf tee, helps to raise the ball, which helps you make better contact with the ball. If you become an accurate, reliable place kicker, you will be a very important member of your team, because successful penalty kicks and conversions keep the scoreboard ticking over. Each international team has a specialist place kicker, who usually practises kicking at least five days a week to develop a kicking routine and almost infallible technique.

Different place kickers place the ball on the tee at different angles and use a variety of approach runs.

We will concentrate on the "round the corner" method. If you do not have a kicking tee, use a marker cone or sand, or just place the ball upright on the ground (you may need to use your heel to make a dent in which to balance the ball). Select your target area, then keep your eyes on the sweet spot of the ball, about a third of the way up the ball (see figure 5.5).

To execute the place kick, place your left foot alongside the ball, and your right foot behind it (for a right footed kicker). Then take three to seven strides back from the ball, and two to the left side. Select your target area, mid-way between the posts and high above the crossbar. Line the ball up with posts, using the seams like gun sights, with one seam facing the posts and one facing you. Visualise the path of flight to the target. Relax, take a couple of deep

Figure 5.5 Locating the sweet spot for place-kicking.

breaths, and focus on success. See the ball soaring between the posts.

Keeping your eyes on the sweet spot of the ball, approach the ball with a balanced, controlled stride (see figure 5.6a). Plant your non-kicking foot alongside the ball with a long last stride. Keep your head down (see figure 5.6b). Keep your weight on your left leg, and make contact with your instep or the top of your big toe while holding your left arm out for balance. To finish the place kick, keep your head down and follow through with a high leg. You are well balanced if your kicking foot settles beside your planted foot.

FIGURE 5.6 **KEYS TO SUCCESS**

PLACE KICK

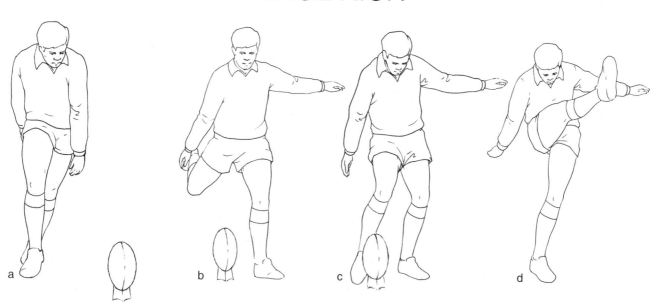

a b c d

Preparation
1. Tee ball up vertically ___
2. Select target between posts, visualise path to target ___
3. Keep eyes on sweet spot ___
4. Line ball up with posts ___
5. Place left foot beside ball, right foot behind it ___
6. Take 3 to 7 paces straight back, 2 to left (for right-footed kick) ___
7. Breathe deep, relax, focus on success ___

Execution
1. Approach ball at slow, steady run ___
2. Plant non-kicking foot beside ball with long, last stride ___
3. Head down ___
4. Left arm out for balance ___
5. Keep kicking foot extended, make contact with instep or top of big toe ___
6. Weight on non-kicking leg ___

Follow-Through
1. Head down after kick ___
2. Kicking leg high and toward posts ___
3. Kicking foot settles beside planted foot ___

How to Catch a Kick

As important as kicking skills is the ability to successfully catch the ball in a controlled manner. To execute the catch properly, keep your eyes on the ball and call "my ball!" to communicate clearly your intentions to your teammates. Then move quickly to the spot where the ball will land, making sure your body is side on to the attackers. Create a wide base by making sure your legs are at least shoulder-width apart to ensure good balance.

Raise your arms, spread your fingers and have relaxed palms facing upward. Catch the ball in your spread fingers and pull the ball down to your chest and arms. As you pull the ball in, sink your hips into a stable, crouched position, sideways to your opponents with your shoulder braced to accept contact. Maintain control of the ball.

FIGURE 5.7

KEYS TO SUCCESS

CATCHING

a

b

c

Preparation

1. Call "my ball", keep eyes on ball ___
2. Move quickly to where ball will land ___
3. Body side on to attackers ___
4. Feet at least shoulder-width apart ___

Execution

1. Raise arms, spread fingers, relaxed palms facing up ___
2. Catch ball in spread fingers ___
3. Pull ball down to chest and arms ___

Follow-Through

1. Sink hips to stable crouch ___
2. Sideways stance with shoulder braced ___
3. Maintain control of ball ___

KICKING SUCCESS STOPPERS

To become an expert kicker takes a long time and requires dedication and concentration. If you experience problems with your new kicking techniques, here are some suggestions for solving some common errors.

Error	Correction
Punt	
1. You throw the ball upward before you kick it and lose control of the ball, resulting in loss of direction and distance.	1. Hold the ball away from you, at about waist height, and bring your foot to the ball. Imagine you are placing the ball on a shelf. Remember to follow through.
2. You have difficulty kicking the ball into touch.	2. Select a target area 5 to 10 metres beyond the touch line; overcompensate to make certain that the ball reaches touch.
3. You keep slicing the ball in the wrong direction.	3. Hit the belly of the ball, and point your toes down to keep a firm kicking foot.
4. You lean backward and lose your balance, which results in a poor punt.	4. Steady yourself if you are on the run, and create a firm base with your non-kicking foot. Keep your head down and your body over the ball.
Grubber Kick	
1. You have difficulty coordinating the movement.	1. Remember to slow down and keep your eyes on the ball, not your opponents, after you have selected the target area.
2. The ball lands awkwardly, so poor contact is made with your foot.	2. Hold the ball across the side seams, with one hand on each side to steady it, and allow it to drop vertically. Try kicking the ball with your instep and side foot for more control.
Drop Kick	
1. You have difficulty controlling the drop of the ball.	1. Hold the ball on each side, with your fingers pointing down or forward, and simply release the ball in front of you.
2. You have difficulty timing the drop and the kick.	2. Relax, and keep your head down and eyes on the ball all the time, especially when it hits the ground.
3. You are unable to get any height on the ball.	3. Your head is coming up too early: Keep it down, and make sure you have a long follow-through with your leg.

Error	Correction
Place Kick	
1. You keep kicking the ball along the ground.	1. Remember to aim for the sweet spot about a third of the way up the ball. You are making contact too high up on the ball, and your non-kicking foot is probably too near the ball.
2. You cannot get the ball to travel in a straight line.	2. Select your target area. You need to concentrate on where you place your non-kicking foot. Ask a friend to point out where you plant your foot. Your foot should land about 20 centimetres behind and 10 centimetres to the side of the ball. Kick through the middle line of the ball, not to the left or right side.
3. You are having trouble kicking the ball far enough.	3. Your last stride may be too long, preventing your kicking foot from swinging through with power. You could be kicking under the ball and making contact too low on the ball.

KICKING

DRILLS

Perfect practice should lead to perfect performance in a game situation, and the following drills are designed to help you achieve kicking success.

1. Punt Kicking for Accuracy

In this drill you work within a four-sectioned grid, each section measuring 8 metres square. You, the punter, stand in grid 1, and your partner stands in grid 3 or 4. Aim to punt the ball accurately to either grid so your partner does not have to move to catch the ball. Ask your partner to change position within the two grid areas after each kick to test your punting accuracy.

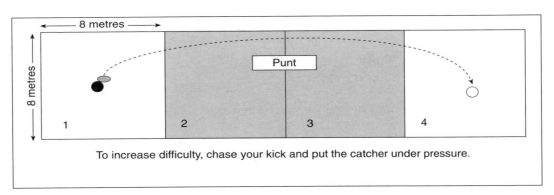

To increase difficulty, chase your kick and put the catcher under pressure.

Success Goal = 10 accurate punts ___

Success Check

• Select target ___
• Keep eyes on ball, head down ___
• Point toes down ___
• Keep both hands under ball ___
• Make contact with top of foot ___

To Increase Difficulty

• Ask a friend to pass you the ball before you kick.
• Pick up a rolling ball, then punt.
• Kick, then chase your ball to put the catcher under pressure.
• Practise punting with your weaker foot.

To Decrease Difficulty

• Use your knee to knock the ball to your partner, who stands 2 metres away.
• Hold the ball with one hand at each end, so that you kick across the long axis and belly of the ball. This should help you control the ball. Practise kicking over one grid to your partner. Remember to kick through the middle of the ball.

2. Up and Under

While you can use the same drills as those suggested for punt kicking for accuracy (drill 1) to help you master the up and under (bomb kick), to further increase the difficulty and effectiveness of your practice, try the following drill. In kicking the bomb, the ball must stay in the air long enough for the chasers to arrive as it comes down. For the chasers to cover 25 metres to get under the kick, the ball needs to be in the air 3.5 seconds. Covering 35 metres requires 5 seconds. Practise accuracy with markers at 25 metres and 35 metres; measure timing (and height) by counting the seconds that the ball is in flight.

Success Goal = 10 accurate punts with correct amount of time in flight ___

Success Check

• Select target ___
• Keep eyes on ball, head down ___
• Point toes down ___
• Keep both hands under ball ___
• Make contact with top of foot ___

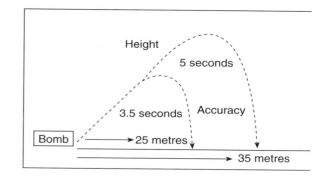

To Increase Difficulty

• Ask a friend to pass you the ball before you kick.
• Pick up a rolling ball, then punt.
• Practise the bomb with your weaker foot.

3. Grubber Kick for Accuracy

Use an area 24 metres long and 8 metres wide divided into three sections. Place cones on the four corners of the work area. Stay in grid 1 and attempt to grubber kick past your partner in grid 3 to score between the two marker cones in grid 3. You and your partner are not allowed in grid 2. Your partner can guard any area he or she chooses in grid 3 to prevent a score. Your partner then attempts to grubber kick the ball past you from where he or she stopped the ball.

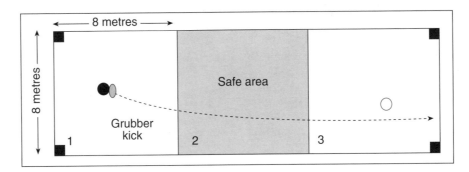

Success Goal = As many goals as you can score in 1 minute ____

Success Check
- Select target ____
- Hold ball upright ____
- Keep head down ____
- Drop ball onto your foot ____
- Punch ball along the ground ____

To Increase Difficulty
- Pick up a ball rolled behind you, turn and immediately grubber kick to beat your partner.

To Decrease Difficulty
- Grubber kick the ball along the ground by using the side (instep) of your foot.

4. Drop Kick for 3 Points

For this drop-kick drill, you make 3 kicks each from 10, 15, and 22 metres directly in front of the posts. Place cones at these distances. Receive a pass from your partner and attempt a drop kick over the bar and between the posts. Remember to keep your eye on the ball and to drop the ball directly onto its point, slightly in front of your kicking foot as you make contact on the half-volley just as the ball rebounds from the ground. Kick straight through the ball and follow through.

Success Goal = 3 successful kicks each from 10, 15, and 22 metres ____

Success Check
- Look at target area ____
- Keep eyes on ball ____
- Drop ball onto its point, slightly in front of kicking foot ____
- Make contact on half-volley just as the ball rebounds from the ground ____
- Kick straight through ball and follow through ____

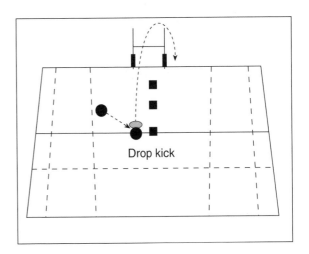

To Increase Difficulty

- Kick with your weaker foot.
- After passing the ball, your partner can run toward you, creating pressure like that of an opposition flanker.
- Move 10 metres to the side at the same distance from the posts to change the angle required of your drop kick.

To Decrease Difficulty

- Take all your drop kicks from 10 metres away.
- Remove the passer, and start in a more controlled, static position with the ball already in your hands when you drop kick.

5. Daily Dozen Place Kicks

Attempt 12 kicks at goal from various distances and angles. Start with three kicks from the 15-metre mark, directly in front of the posts. Remember to practise good place-kicking form: Line the ball up, keep your eyes on the sweet spot, approach the ball under control, and swing through and beyond the ball.

Success Goal = 7 successful kicks out of 12 ___

Success Check
- Line up ball ___
- Keep eyes on sweet spot ___
- Approach ball under control ___
- Plant non-kicking foot alongside ball ___
- Head down ___
- Swing through and beyond ball ___

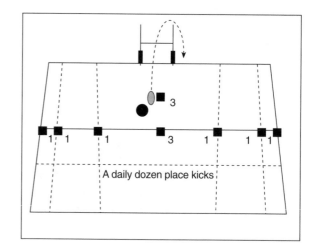

A daily dozen place kicks

To Increase Difficulty

- Use your weaker foot for all 12 kicks.
- Increase the distance from the posts.

To Decrease Difficulty

- Take all 12 place kicks from the 15-metre mark in front of the posts.

KICKING SUCCESS SUMMARY

You will have a lot of fun learning to kick accurately. Set yourself high standards and lots of challenges. Initially concentrate on perfecting technique, then accuracy and finally power. Remember that good kicking wins games, and poor kicking loses games, but be patient with yourself. Kicking over the approaching defence is one way of getting the ball over the gain line and in front of your players. It's important that you and your team communicate and know when, why and where you are going to kick to help your chasers to regain possession and put your opponents under pressure. You have to learn what type of kick is required for any given situation in a match.

You may find in the early stages of learning to kick that what you learn inhibits your natural ability. However, as you master the various techniques, your naturalness will come through, and you and a teammate or coach can check your Keys to Success fundamentals against the checklists in figures 5.1 through 5.7. Remember to keep your head down and your eyes on the ball and to practise with both feet for distance, height and accuracy.

STEP

6 CONTACT: CONTROLLING CONTINUITY

It might not seem like it to you when you are watching or playing a game of rugby, but most of the time players are attempting to avoid contact. Your aim should be to use contact as a last resort, and you should view ruck and maul situations as continuity failures, failures to keep the ball moving forward. In reality, your sidestep, swerve and passing skills will ultimately lead to some sort of contact. You will find yourself in contact with opponents, your own teammates and the ground. You need to prepare for and know how to make contact with opponents on your terms, with your body and the ball under control, to ensure that your team keeps possession.

You have to decide whether to pass or present the ball before, during or after contact. Your decision is based on the shape of the defence in front of you and the positioning of your support players.

In Step 4 we concentrated on tackling and how to stop your opponents from progressing down the playing field. Here we will look at ways of keeping possession of the ball and using the ball in contact situations—techniques such as the bump, gut pass, ruck and maul—to remain in control of the game. You will need to practise these techniques with your teammates to learn to understand each other's body language and to react to produce a coordinated sequence of support movements, which enables your team to keep controlled possession of the ball.

During the game you may find yourself attempting to drive through the opposition or supporting the drive of a teammate who has made contact. Sometimes the contact with your teammates is as forceful as the contact you make with the opposition, because you wish to ensure that you retain possession of the ball and keep the ball moving forward against a determined defence. If you remain straight legged and upright, you will make no impact on the opposition.

Imagine you are pushing your family car that has run out of petrol. Your body position would be low, with shoulders higher than your hip level, head up, knees bent and legs driving hard. It's important to stay on your feet to prevent toppling over and landing flat on your face. The principles are similar for making contact in rugby.

To maintain the continuity of your attack, as the ball carrier you must find your support, and your support players must try hard to stay close to you. If you are the first support player to arrive at a ball on the ground, you can either pick it up and run forward, pick it up and pass, secure the ball for your team or stop the opposition from getting the ball.

Every player on your team regardless of position needs to have the knowledge and technique to maximise the benefit to your team from contact situations such as tackling, rucking and mauling. You need to develop confidence by systematically practising contact techniques in a safe environment, so that they become a natural part of your game. You may wish the defender to hold a tackle shield, although it is better if you make body-to-body contact. At this beginner, learning stage the defender should not interfere with the ball and must take a wide stance with one shoulder pointing toward you, so that there will be some resistance when you make contact. You need to be thoroughly warmed up before you start your contact practice with a partner.

At some point in a game you will inevitably make contact with the ground, and you need to learn to fall safely. We will look at falling in this chapter as well. The state of the pitch will change depending on the weather: Sometimes it will be wet, soggy and muddy, and at other times dry, hard and with little grass cover. There's nothing like a hard pitch to keep you on your feet!

How to Execute the Bump

As the ball carrier, you have a range of options if you are about to make contact with an opponent. The first to consider is the bump.

As you near the defender, begin to lead with one shoulder, lower your body toward the ground and push the ball back and away from the contact area, still holding it in two hands. Just before you make contact, take a long, low last stride and bump up and into your opponent's shoulder. If you make a very strong contact, your opponent will step backward a short distance; this will create time and space for you to pop pass the ball to your support player.

If you have created enough space with the bump, use your front leg as a pivot, roll your back toward your opponent, swing your rear heel through 180 degrees and drive powerfully off that foot past the defender. You should then link up with your nearest team member.

How to Execute the Gut Pass

If you have been weaving slightly from side to side to prevent the defender from remaining in one place, you can use a gut pass. You should make a long, low, last stride into shoulder-to-shoulder contact, drive up and into the defender and roll your back to any further contact (see figure 6.1a). Use your front foot as a pivot and turn through a quarter of a circle until you can see your support (see figure 6.1b). From this position, you are ready to use the gut pass to move the ball to your support player.

Move the ball away from your chest in two hands, and push the ball firmly up and in to the lower chest region of your support player (see figure 6.1c). The support player must lean in to the ball by lowering his or her shoulders, reach out with one hand over and one below the ball and follow it to the chest with his or her hands. The support player should stay low and drive beyond the defender.

FIGURE 6.1 **KEYS TO SUCCESS**

GUT PASS

a

Preparation

1. Lead defender away from where you intend to deliver the ball ____
2. Lower shoulder and bend knees slightly ____

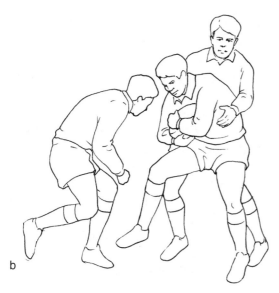

b

Execution

1. With long, low, last stride, bump up and into opponent's lower chest ___
2. Make contact with shoulder so ball remains visible to support ___
3. Do not try to knock defender over—just make contact ___
4. Push ball backward as you go ___

c

Follow-Through

1. Push or pass ball into support's hands ___
2. Support player reaches one hand over, one hand under ball ___
3. Remain strong in contact area by maintaining a wide base ___
4. Support new ball carrier immediately ___

Employing the Ruck and Maul

There are so many variables in a game of rugby—and situations change so rapidly—that you need to make instant decisions to best help your team. You need to be clear about the possibilities and difficulties associated with employing ruck and maul contact techniques.

A ruck is formed when the ball is on the ground and one or more players from each team are on their feet and in physical contact, closing around the ball between them. A ruck is a technique used by a group of your teammates to retain or regain possession, usually when one team member has been tackled in open play, away from the line-out or scrum set piece. A maul is formed by one or more players from each team on their feet and in physical contact closing round a player who is in possession of the ball.

In some situations it will be better to ruck because you are trying to disorganise the defence and retain or obtain the ball in a tackle situation. A ruck produces early ball in an attacking situation, is more dynamic than a maul and keeps you going forward, is technically simpler for your support players and helps your backs to time their runs because they can often see the ball coming out. However, it is difficult to ruck unless you are going forward, and the ball is often more difficult to control, especially for scrum halves passing from the ground.

In contrast, you may decide to maul during a game rather than ruck because you are retreating and need to recover control of the ball or because your attack has been partially halted by the opposition. You can also use a maul as a deliberate ploy to disorganise the defence. Mauls can produce problems if they are static, and a slow ball is produced in attacking situations if too many players get their hands on the ball. It is important to have good decision makers on your team to maul effectively.

How to Execute the Ruck

To ruck well your players usually need to arrive at the contact or tackle situation before the opposition and then drive forward. To disorganise a defence and keep the ball moving forward quickly, it's good to set up a dynamic and fast ruck to produce early ball. If you are the ball carrier, you should first make contact with your leading shoulder and attempt to bump the tackler away (see figure 6.2a). If you are held, turn toward your support. Go to the ground slowly to buy time for your support. As you hit the ground, place the ball at arm's length behind you so it is closer to your support. Then place your hands over your ears, elbows up, to protect your head (see figure 6.2b).

Support players should drive over the top of tackled player and ball and bind onto (wrap their arms around and grip tightly to) opposition or another support player (see figure 6.2c). If you are a support player, drive forward with a low body position, keeping your eyes open, your head looking forward, with your chin off your chest. Keep your back flat, your body heading toward the goal line and your shoulders always above your hips. Shrug your shoulders, and keep your neck loose on contact. Stay on your feet, and keep your opponents on their feet (see figure 6.2d).

The ball carrier needs to get back up on his or her feet quickly to prepare to support the next piece of play once the support passes over. The support and driving players need to assess the situation and move to offer their support at the next stoppage or to join in the passing movement once the ball has been passed away from the ruck.

| FIGURE 6.2 | KEYS TO SUCCESS |

THE RUCK

a

b

Preparation

Ball carrier:
1. Make contact with leading shoulder ____
2. Try to bump tackler away ____
3. If held, turn toward your support ____
4. Go to ground slowly ____
5. Place ball at arm's length behind you, closer to support ____
6. Place hands over ears, elbows up, to protect your head ____

Execution

Support players:

1. Drive over top of tackled player ___
2. Bind onto the opposition or another support player ___
3. Drive low, eyes open, head looking forward ___
4. Keep back flat and shoulders always above hips ___
5. Shrug shoulders and loosen neck on contact ___
6. Stay on your feet, keep opponents on their feet ___

Follow-Through

1. Ball carrier gets to feet quickly ___
2. Support players move to next stoppage or join in passing movement ___

Figure 6.3 Go with the impact.

Sometimes you will not be able to stop the defender tackling you to the ground, and your support will be too far away for you to pass the ball. To execute the ruck in this situation, you need to place the ball under control on the ground, to allow your nearest support player to pick it up, or drive over it and into the opposition, before your team loses possession.

When preparing to make contact with the ground it is important to go with the flow of the impact of the tackle as this will help you to land and roll naturally. You should attempt to round your shoulder, and land mainly on your back and side (see figure 6.3a). Bend your knees, keep tucked up, and do not put a straight arm or hand out to break your fall. Tuck your chin into your chest as you land (see figure 6.3b).

You can attempt to create rucks that have a particular balanced shape or structure, depending on the actions of the ball carrier and first support player.

A 2-3-2 ruck (see diagram 6.1) is created when, because of close support players, the ball carrier decides to place the ball on the ground just before or as contact is made. The two support players get low, bind on early and drive in on either side of the ball carrier. The next three players bind on and form a wider driving base. A 2-3-2 ruck also occurs when the ball is already on the ground, usually after a tackle, with an opponent trying to get the ball. If two support players arrive together, they should get low,

bind onto each other and the opposition and drive the opposition out of the way to free the ball, with the help of your other support players as they arrive at the breakdown (tackle situation).

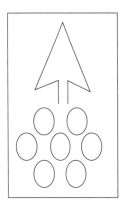

Diagram 6.1 A 2-3-2 ruck when the ball is already on the ground.

A 3-2-3 ruck (see diagram 6.2) is created when the ball carrier is on his or her feet in contact, and it appears that the opposition is getting their hands on the ball. The first support player decides to change the maul situation into a ruck situation by ripping the ball from the ball carrier, going to the ground and releasing the ball for the support players to drive over and the scrum half to pass away.

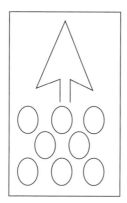

Diagram 6.2 A 3-2-3 shape when ball carrier goes to the ground.

How to Execute the Maul

The ball carrier is the most important person in the maul, because his or her initial contact affects everyone else's reactions. By keeping the ball in your hands and off the ground, you present a target for your support players. To execute the maul, drop your chin to your chest for protection as you make contact with the point of your leading shoulder (see figure 6.4a). Shrug your shoulders on contact and drive from a low position up into the opponent's midriff. Step to the side of your opponent to unbalance him or her and turn slightly sideways as you hold the ball firmly to your chest with two hands. Bend your knees and establish a wide, solid base to stay on your feet (see figure 6.4b). Keep driving with your legs while keeping the ball visible to your first support player. Get a pass away to the support player if you can.

When you drive into the opposition, do not get isolated or turned toward your opponents. You often rely on the nearest player in your team to support you quickly, so your team has four protective hands on the ball (see figure 6.4c). The support player should keep his or her eyes open and look at the ball. He or she should drive in under the ball and upward, keeping shoulders square to the goal lines, and use the shoulder opposite to the ball carrier to create a barrier (see figure 6.4d). The support player has four basic choices:

1. To strip or take the ball and run on with it
2. To strip or take the ball and pass to another supporting player
3. To secure and isolate the ball with the ball carrier and buy time for the next support player
4. To stop the opposition from having the ball

The rest of your supporting players need to drive the maul forward, protect the ball, and keep everyone (including the opposition) on their feet (see figure 6.4e). Move the ball to the back of the maul if the opposition prevents a roll around the edge of the maul, and try to release the ball to your scrum half while you are still driving forward (see figure 6.4f).

FIGURE
6.4

KEYS TO SUCCESS

THE MAUL

Preparation

Ball carrier:
1. Eyes open and head up ___
2. Take a long, low, last stride before contact ___
3. Keep low ___
4. Body weight over leading foot ___
5. Drop chin to chest for protection ___

Support player:
1. Eyes open and on ball ___
2. Drive under ball and upward ___
3. Shoulders square to goal lines ___
4. Shoulder opposite to ball carrier creates barrier ___

Execution

Ball carrier:
1. Step to opponent's side to unbalance him or her ___
2. Make contact with point of leading shoulder ___
3. Drive low up into opponent's midriff ___
4. Hold ball firmly on chest with two hands ___
5. Shrug shoulders on contact, turn slightly sideways ___
6. Look forward, keep driving with legs ___
7. Keep ball visible to support player ___

Support players:
1. Share ball with ball carrier: 4 hands on ball ___
2. One arm over top and one underneath ball ___
3. Drive together, legs moving ___
4. You and opponents on feet, protect ball ___

e

Follow-Through

1. Communicate with each other ___
2. Take or "uncouple" ball and pass, run or roll out, staying on feet, and pivoting on leading shoulder ___
3. Move ball to back if opposition prevents roll around the edge ___
4. Release ball to scrum half while driving forward ___

f

CONTACT SUCCESS STOPPERS

Learning to execute both a ruck and a maul is easier if you can compare correct and incorrect techniques. The most common ruck and maul errors are listed here, along with suggestions to help you correct them.

Error	Correction
Ruck: Ball Carrier	
1. You are turned as you go to the ground.	1. Drive your tackler back, then go to the ground under control.
2. You lose control of the ball as you attempt to place it on the ground.	2. Concentrate on landing on your side, not on the ball. Practice placing the ball with both hands.
3. You get knocked on the head after you place the ball.	3. Protect your head with your hands and elbows after you have placed the ball.
4. You present the ball before your support arrives.	4. Slow down if your support is too far away.

Error	Correction
Ruck: Support Players	
1. You keep falling over.	1. Stay on your feet, look forward and keep your shoulders above your hips. Bind onto a teammate or the opposition with a firm grip.
2. As you make contact, you come to a halt.	2. Keep pumping and driving your legs quickly.
3. You arrive at an angle and drive across the pitch toward the touch line.	3. As you arrive at the ruck, get your spine in line with the touch lines, and drive straight down the length of the pitch to force the opposition backward.
Maul: Ball Carrier	
1. You drive in too far and get isolated from your support.	1. Bump the tackler away and recoil to create time and space for your support players.
2. You aim for middle of your opponent and smother the ball.	2. Make contact with your opponent's side to unbalance him or her.
3. You get turned toward opposition.	3. Your last stride should be long and low so you can sink your hips, bend your knees and make a wide, solid base with your feet and legs.
4. You lose control of the ball as you make contact.	4. If a pass is not possible as you make contact, hold the ball firmly close to your chest with two hands until your support arrives.
5. You fall over when you release the ball.	5. After releasing the ball, use your arms to hold up the support player and keep you both on your feet.
Maul: Support Players	
1. You take your eyes off the ball.	1. Focus on the ball as a target.
2. You drive in too high above the ball and have no impact.	2. Drive in and under the ball. Keep low.
3. You use the same shoulder as the carrier, and don't block off the ball from the opposition.	3. When you drive in to secure the ball, lead with the shoulder opposite to the ball carrier.

CONTACT

DRILLS

1. Falling Under Control

In a grid 8 metres by 8 metres, follow your partner, who calls "down". Both of you practise falling gradually, then getting up quickly. Now repeat the practice holding a ball, which you place under control at arm's length to the side of your body when you fall. The ball should remain still for your teammate to pick up easily.

Success Goal = 5 falls with ball well placed ___

Success Check
• Do not use arms to break fall, or fall with limbs extended ___
• Tighten and round landing shoulder ___
• Ball is last to hit the ground ___

To Increase Difficulty
• After you have placed the ball, your partner straddles the ball or you, lifts the ball, runs forward for 5 paces, then falls down, and you switch roles. Get up quickly to get back into the game after your partner has lifted the ball.

To Decrease Difficulty
• Start on your knees, then fall to the ground, placing the ball carefully for your teammate to pick up.

2. Drive and Protect

Use an 8 metre by 8 metre grid. A partner provides initially passive, controlled defence, so you get used to making contact with the opposition. Pick up a ball, walk to the side of your partner, and make contact. Your partner acting as a defender holds you up. Your partner checks your technique and gives you feedback and marks (on a scale of 10) for each attempt.

Progress to playing a 1 vs. 1 walking game across your 8 metre grid. Start with the ball on your goal line, go forward, and attempt to drive your partner backward and score over his or her goal line. Your partner can tackle you to the ground. When you are tackled to the ground, both you and your partner have to get up quickly and regain your feet before you can play the ball again. Your partner can also rip the ball out of your hands.

Success Goal = 3 successful attempts with left shoulder, 3 with right ___

Success Check
• Keep shoulders above hips ___
• Keep eyes open ___
• Make a long, low, last stride ___
• Hold ball firmly ___
• Turn slightly sideways to protect ball ___
• Drive legs parallel to touch line ___

To Increase Difficulty
• Play a 1 vs. 1 jogging or full-speed game across an 8 metre by 8 metre grid or a 16 metre long by 8 metre wide grid.

To Decrease Difficulty
• Your partner stands still, holding the ball. You practise picking up and turning your partner. Use your legs rather than your back to lift. Another good practice is for you to face your partner and allow him or her to drive you across the grid, then change over on the way back. You can attempt this with or without a ball.

3. Continuity Practice

Work in a grid area 10 metres long by 5 metres wide, with three players attacking against one passive defender. You cannot pass the ball before contact. Attack the edge of the defender, drive forward, then gradually sink to the ground, placing the ball at arm's length away from you. The first support player drives over you and the ball in a low body position, making contact with the defender and leaving the ball behind for the second support player to pick up and score over the goal line. Start the practice at jogging pace until you get used to it to ensure safety.

Success Goal = 5 successful tries each with right and left shoulders ____

Success Check

Ball carrier:
- Select target ____
- Long, low, last stride ____
- Drive forward, then turn to support ____
- Gradually sink to ground ____
- Place ball at arm's length ____

Support player:
- Eyes open, looking forward ____
- Get low early, keep shoulders above hips ____
- Drive over top of ball carrier and ball ____
- Bind on and drive opposition backward ____
- Stay on your feet ____

To Increase Difficulty
- You choose to set up either a maul, ruck or pass before, during or after contact. The support players have to learn to read your body language and react quickly. Start at jogging pace, and when you feel confident, try the activity at different running speeds.

To Decrease Difficulty
- Start lying on the ground in front of a defender and place the ball on the ground. The first support player jogs out and gently drives over you and the ball.
- The ball carrier sets up a maul position in the tackle. When the first support player arrives, they get four hands on the ball and drive forward together, then the first support player slowly goes to the ground, leaving the initial player standing as a barrier against the opposition. This creates more time for the third support player to arrive to help you.

4. Driving 2 vs. 1 and 3 vs. 1

Work in a 10 metre by 5 metre grid. The ball carrier picks up the ball, which is half-way between the support player and the defender, and jogs to make contact with the defender's side. The support player arrives, ensures that four hands are on the ball and drives forward through the area with the initial ball carrier to score.

The 3 vs. 1 drill uses the same techniques as the 2 vs. 1 drill, but a second support player helps by binding into the gap between the players or over the back of the first ball carrier. All three attackers attempt to drive the ball through the grid area to score over the goal line. Remember to stay on your feet. After achieving success goals, exchange positions.

Success Goal = As many tries as possible from 2 attempts, 1 each with right and left shoulders ____

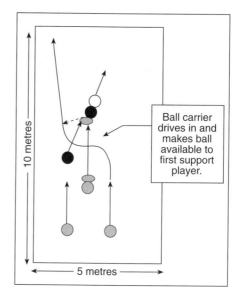

✔ Success Check

Ball carrier:
- Make contact with leading shoulder ___
- Bump up and into defender ___
- Hold ball away from contact area as support arrives ___
- Turn slightly sideways and shrug shoulders ___

First support player:
- Drive in and under ball ___
- Use shoulder opposite to ball carrier ___
- Share ball with ball carrier ___
- Drive together ___

Second support player:
- Bind over, not onto, first ball carrier, or fill the gap and drive ___
- Drive legs, keeping shoulders above hips ___
- Keep spine in line with touch lines ___
- Be ready to receive a pass from first support player ___

Ball carrier drives in and makes ball available to first support player.

To Increase Difficulty

- Play a 3 vs. 2 or 2 vs. 2 walking, driving and tackling game across a 16 metre long by 8 metre wide grid. If tackled, you have to release the ball for others to pick up, unless you get back on your feet quickly to play the ball again. Experiment with pivoting, turning, and rolling around the defenders, then driving straight. Keep in close contact with your support players and work as a team, sometimes holding each other up.

To Decrease Difficulty

- Play a 1 vs. 1 keep ball game. Both of you have to stay on your feet and in the grid. You have to wrestle the ball away from your partner by pulling down on the ball when they pull up, and vice versa, or by getting your hands between your partner's elbows and the ball and pulling down.

CONTACT SUCCESS SUMMARY

In contesting for possession of the ball, you will inevitably make contact. As you practise the suggested drills, contact will become a natural part of your game, and you will make a significant contribution to your team effort. Remember that losing possession allows your opponents the opportunity to attack, but also that the main aim of rugby is to avoid contact and keep the ball moving forward, and score tries. Rucks and mauls are temporary stoppages, but necessary techniques to master to ensure that you retain possession when halted in your progress down the field.

Always practise contact work with someone the same size as you, and help each other to learn by being patient. Gradually progress from standing, to walking, to jogging and finally to running. By being sensible and learning the correct contact techniques, you will make contact in practice and game situations safe, effective and enjoyable. Don't forget to assess your progress in contact skills by using the Keys to Success items in figures 6.1 and 6.2. Have fun, and remember that if you "keep your spine in line, your drive will be fine", and if you "stay on your feet, the opposition will retreat".

THE FRONT FIVE: THE PROVIDERS

There are 15 players in each team: 8 forwards and 7 backs. These large units can be further separated into smaller ones consisting of the front five, middle five and back five players. Each player within the unit has a range of specialist roles to play, especially the front five at scrum and line-out. These are ways of bringing the ball back into play and are commonly referred to as "set pieces".

The purpose of the scrum is to bring the ball back into play after the attack fails due to an infringement and the opponents are unable to take advantage. The line-out brings the ball back into play after it or a player carrying it has left the field of play. In these situations, responsibility falls on the front five to gain possession for the team. This chapter deals with the roles of the front five: the ball providers.

The positions of the front five unit are the loose-head prop, the hooker, the tight-head prop and the two locks. These players are the primary ball winners in the scrum and the line-out. Because of the possibility of injury to players during contact at the set piece there are a number of safety factors which must be considered, particularly at the scrum.

Safety Factors and Body Positioning for the Scrum

There are many safety factors that the front unit must understand and that the referee must enforce for both teams. The laws demand that you make contact with the opposition in a very controlled way:

- Props and locks must crouch after the referee has indicated that the scrums can engage. Touch your opposite number, pause and engage the opposition front row.
- The force of this first contact should go slightly upward to prevent a collapse.

- Props should keep hips square and outside foot slightly forward.
- Your inside hip should remain as close to the centre of the scrummage as possible, with your inside foot almost touching that of your other prop's.
- The thigh of the inner leg should be almost vertical so that your knee is never ahead of your hip.
- Keep a wide stance by making sure your feet are as flat on the ground as possible.

All players in the scrum must adopt a safe scrummaging position (see figure 7.1).

- Head up, chin off chest and back flat
- Legs bent slightly at the knees
- Shoulders always above hips

Prop Forwards

There are two prop forwards in each unit. In the scrum, the prop forwards' main role is to provide a

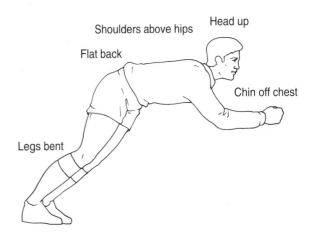

Shoulders above hips   Head up

Flat back

Chin off chest

Legs bent

Figure 7.1   Head up, chin off chest and back

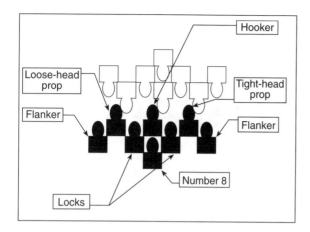

Diagram 7.1　Players in the scrum.

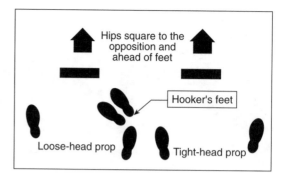

Diagram 7.2　Strong, square position.

solid platform and support for the hooker to win quick and controlled ball. The loose-head prop forward plays on the left-hand side of the front row and the tight-head prop on the right (see diagram 7.1).

There is always a great deal of force directed at props, so they must be strong and enjoy contact. Normally to play prop you should have a short neck and broad shoulders because the force of the scrum goes through the props' spines into the opposition. Being particularly strong in the arms, back and chest also helps, as will very strong legs—most of your scrummaging stability comes from your thighs and buttocks. You will absorb much of the opposition's drive with your legs and should take short, backward steps only if absolutely necessary. Remember to always keep your weight just in front of your stance.

Nowadays props play a very important role after their positional responsibilities at the scrummage and in the line-out have finished. You must be able to contribute to the attacking and defensive potential of the team.

Positional Requirements

As the prop forward, these are your main priorities:

At the Scrum

- Provide a solid platform for your hooker to win good ball.
- As a loose head, resist the force from the opposition and support the hooker in every way.
- As a tight head, hold a strong, square position (see diagram 7.2).

At the Line-Out

- Support the jumper in the jump-and-catch sequence.
- Quickly close in on the jumper to shut off any gaps.
- Protect any ball that may have been secured.
- If required, take the ball from the jumper in order to give it back to the scrum half or peel around the back of the line-out.
- On the opposition throw, it is your role as a prop to try to go through any gaps that may occur after they win the ball, so that you put pressure on the opposition's possession (see diagram 7.3).
- If the opportunity arises, try to take the ball from the opposition jumper.

In the Loose

- In contact you must stay on your feet, keep the ball and resist the opposition.

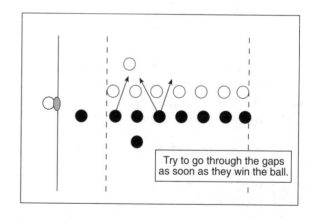

Try to go through the gaps as soon as they win the ball.

Diagram 7.3　Put pressure on the opposition's ball.

- You must drive in dynamically at rucks and mauls with a good body position.

- At kick-offs you must move quickly to any player who is about to catch the ball and to help secure it.

- Occasionally you may have to enter a contact situation and wrestle the ball out.

- You must contribute to the team's tackle count.

- You must understand what you are trying to achieve from all areas of play.

How to Position for the Scrum

In the scrum a good, safe body position is vital. It is against the laws of the game to allow your shoulders to go below your hips. The golden rules of scrummaging are head up, chin off chest, flat back, shoulders above hips, legs bent, wide stance, feet as flat as possible (see figure 7.1). You should practise this position against a suitably adjusted scrummaging machine and progress to working against other players.

To position correctly you should bind tightly with a wide stance and your outside foot slightly forward. Crouch and sight where you will put your head. Engage your opponent firmly, drive slightly upward, with your hips and shoulders square. Settle quickly, then keep movement to a minimum. Remember to keep your shoulders always above your hips. Remain static, with your shoulders horizontal. As soon as the ball is won, rejoin the support as quickly as possible.

Supporting Jumpers at Kick-Off and Line-Out

In the line-out, one of the props normally stands at the front and the other third in line. The jumper will normally stand between you. Your role is to help protect the jumper during the contest for possession of the ball.

Safety is most important. Supporting the jumper should only take place once the player has touched the ball and ought to be concentrated on bringing the player down from the jump under control. At the line-out you should play in a head-up position to watch the ball reach the jumper.

Many supporting actions at a kick-off are very similar to those used at the line-out. The major difference is that at kick-off players are able to move a

Figure 7.2 Support and control the landing.

greater distance. Once the jumper is in the air you can safely support and control the landing. Beware of taking hold of the player too early, which leads to instability. If you hold the player above waist level, you should find that all landings are safe and under control (see figure 7.2).

In practice you will choose to support for either a line-out or kick-off. In many ways the support is very similar. As soon as the jumper moves to catch the ball, react to the situation and play on. Your options are simple:

- Drive forward and bind onto the jumper.

- Drive on to the jumper, strip the ball away and pass the ball away to the scrum half or another player.

- Drive forward, strip the ball away and carry on driving.

- Drive forward, strip the ball and immediately give it to someone in a better position to continue the attack than you.

Hooker

The hooker is one of the main ball winners on the team. In the scrum the hooker wins the ball by striking it down the channel between the left side prop's feet and back into the scrum to finish up at the feet of the number 8. In the line-out the hooker is responsible for the throw-in from touch. Players in this position can be almost any shape or size, but in general it helps to have a short back and long arms to help bind around the props (see diagram 7.1).

Positional Requirements

These are the main priorities of the hooker:

At the Scrum

- Make sure that you always win your ball by striking it cleanly down the target channel.
- Put pressure on the opposition's put-in.

At the Line-Out

- Throw accurately to the jumpers.
- Help protect any ball that has been won or tidy up any loose ball.
- Pose a constant threat around the front of the line-out to the opposition's throw.
- Defend the narrow attacking side after the line-out has ended.

In the Loose

- When necessary, play as a defender in rucks and mauls.
- Contribute to your team's tackle count.
- Mark the open side of the field at kick-offs.
- Drive in dynamically at rucks and mauls with a good body position.
- Understand and involve yourself in attacking and defensive roles in all areas of the field and in all situations.

Binding for the Scrum

When binding for the scrum, the hooker has a number of options. The rugby laws dictate that hookers may bind over or under the arms of their props, around their body below or at armpit level (see figure 7.3). There is no doubt that the most effective way is to bind both arms over those of the props. The loose head should bind first and must bind around your body onto your waist or middle chest. You may have a preference, which the front row should adopt. The tight head also has a choice of binding onto you:

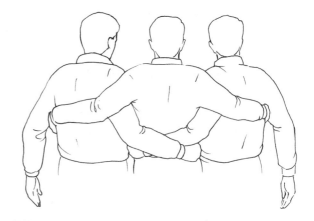

Figure 7.3 Bind both arms over those of the props.

around your body, over the arm of the loose head, from your left hip to your mid-chest.

At the scrum you make contact with your opponents in exactly the same way as your props (see preceding section on prop forwards). You should pull firmly with your left arm and allow your weight to rest on your right (see figure 7.4). Although you are allowed to turn your feet to point toward the mouth of the tunnel, in the scrum you must not move your feet so far to your left that you cause instability in the front row; and should retain a hooking position at all times. Remember that your shoulders must always be above your hips.

You are always in a vulnerable position in the scrum because you are hanging between two other

Figure 7.4 Pull firmly with your left arm.

players with your body ever so slightly turned to face the mouth of the tunnel. Be sure to practise good body positioning at all times.

How to Execute the Hook

To execute the hook, first settle early in the scrum, feet pointing slightly toward the mouth of the tunnel, hips lower than the props'. Look for the scrum half's hands. Your striking foot must be in contact with the ground. Signal for the ball. As the ball leaves scrum half's hands, strike it back through the target channel. Complete the leg sweep and retake a firm stance. Contribute to any push in the scrum. Leave the scrum with the rest of the front row and rejoin in the support of the ball as soon as possible.

When you play hooker, you develop your own style of hooking. This will depend on the quality of your props and also your flexibility, size and leg length. You will strike for the ball only with your right foot. Your aim is to strike the ball in front of and beyond the loose-head prop's leg as soon as possible after it leaves the scrum half's hands. Your target channel is between the feet of the loose-head prop (see diagram 7.4).

There are three basic techniques for hooking:

1. A sweep with the inside side of the foot (see diagram 7.4)
2. A stab and drag, with the sole of the boot or the inside edge (see diagram 7.5)
3. A stab and hit, normally with the heel (see diagram 7.6)

To practise your hooking technique, find some way of resting on your right arm at the correct height for

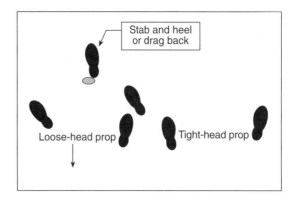

Diagram 7.5   Use the sole of the boot.

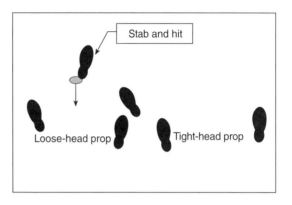

Diagram 7.6   Hit with the heel.

the scrummage. This may be a low wall, an exercise bar or the side of the scrummaging machine. Take the weight on your right forearm, sink your hips toward the ground, and place your feet outside your left shoulder along the ground to simulate the hooking position. This will allow you to practise effectively.

As you grow older, increasing the speed of your strike will become less and less important, because the props in senior rugby are strong enough to protect the possession and will not succumb to the pressure exerted by your opponents. Your strike however, will always need to be fast and firm. Remember, at every one of your own scrums you have the advantage because the ball is put into the scrummage from your left and you are half a body nearer to the mouth of the tunnel than your opponent (see diagram 7.7). You also have the advantage of using your right leg and its joints in their natural range of movement—your opponent hasn't. You will soon learn to use this advantage so that your scrummage ball is rarely threatened.

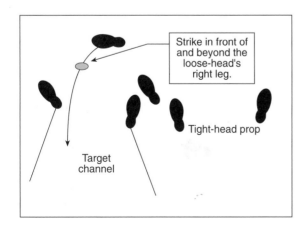

Diagram 7.4   Sweep with the inside sole of your right foot.

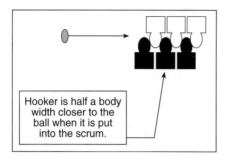

Hooker is half a body width closer to the ball when it is put into the scrum.

Diagram 7.7 Ball put in from the left.

As soon as you have mastered some of the hooking techniques, it is time to try them out against another front row. Although at first it may seem very uncomfortable to have someone else's bony shoulder resting across the back of your neck, you will soon become used to this and accept it as one of the pleasures of front row play.

How to Execute the Line-Out Throw

To execute the line-out throw, hold the ball near the back point across the seams in both hands behind your head, with the ball pointing down the line of touch (i.e., perpendicular to the touch line; see figure 7.5). Stand with one foot forward and the other back. Look at a point above the jumper to where you will throw the ball. Move both hands forward to throw, keeping your hands on the ball for as long as possible. Release the ball as your body weight moves forward (see figure 7.5c). Step onto the field as you release the ball to follow the action and support the new ball carrier.

FIGURE 7.5 **KEYS TO SUCCESS**

LINE-OUT THROW

a   b   c

Preparation

1. Hold ball across seam near back point, pointing down line of touch ____
2. Hold ball behind head in 2 hands; one foot forward, the other back ____
3. Look above jumper to where you will throw ____

Execution

1. Move both hands forward to throw ____
2. Keep hands on ball as long as possible ____
3. Release as body weight moves forward ____

Follow-Through

1. Step onto field as you release ball ____
2. Follow action to support new ball carrier ____

A jumper may come forward or backward to jump or may jump straight up and down. You must establish a range of signals which the jumper will use to let you know the type of jump which he will use to try to win possession. You may wish to practise individually with the jumpers, but as soon as possible, the props should join in so that they too can practise their line-out skills. Your jumpers must always stand away from you, the distance from the touch line they will in the match, so that you can concentrate on accuracy.

To increase accuracy you must take time alone to practise all your throws. Use targets that are available to you. Mark out a series of lines on the ground at the same distance from you as the jumper would be in a line-out. For a low, flat throw, you should aim at either a goal post or a line at the correct height on a wall. For a lob throw, aim at a basketball or netball ring and try to drop the ball down into the basket.

Practise the skills you will use in the game: Your lock may wish to catch or to tap the ball down so that you can practise gathering untidy possession, for example the ball may richochet out of the line-out and onto the ground nearby—if you don't get there first then the opposition hooker might. Cleaning up is another of your major roles at the front of the line-out, and it must become instinctive, even in practice.

Lock

The priorities of the two locks are to win the ball in the line-out and push in the scrum. Locks are normally noted for their height and power. If you are tall, strong, have good basketball skills and enjoy contact, you may be the ideal player for this position.

When you practise scrummaging, you should first experiment with your foot positioning to see which placement will generate the most force and also give excellent resistance to the opposition's drive. A scrummage machine that measures force will help you to compare the different forces that you can exert.

Positional Requirements

These are the lock's main priorities:

In the Scrum

- Provide solid support for the front row.
- Exert power forward when required.
- Resist the opposition's shove.
- Show a safe scrummaging position at all times.
- Bind tightly to both lock and prop throughout the scrummage.

In the Line-Out

- Win the ball when it is thrown to you as the jumper.
- Compete vigorously against your opponent.

In the Loose

- Catch or control any kick-off that comes to you.
- Drive in dynamically at rucks and mauls with a safe body position.
- Rip out any available ball in rucks and mauls.
- Contribute to your team's tackle count.
- Understand and involve yourself in attacking and defensive roles in all areas of the field and in all situations.

How to Position for the Scrum

There are a number of ways you can bind with your partner in the second row, but the most frequently used is the bind across and down onto the outside hip, at waist level so that you pull each other's inside hips close together. If you are playing on the left of the scrum, you should bind under the arm and around the body of the right-side lock. By binding in this way, you will create a little more space for your hooker because your right shoulder is moved slightly backward in the scrum. Your outside shoulder should fit neatly under the buttock of your prop, and your outside arm should reach as far round the outside of the prop's hip as possible.

When you bind up with your teammates ready to go into the scrum you should bind with your lock partner first and then squat down behind the front row and bind onto them. For immediate stability your feet should already be in a wide, stable position, one foot slightly ahead of the other, legs slightly bent at the knee. If you prefer to scrummage both feet back you may have to squat, one foot up, one foot back; you can then start by kneeling down on the back knee. If you scrummage both feet back and you find it uncomfortable to squat, you can go down on one knee; at the moment you make contact, you slide your foot back into position.

When the referee gives you the signal to engage, you should extend your legs and stay strong while both front rows make firm contact. It is essential that you move your feet and legs as little as possible and that you maintain a safe scrummaging position: head up, back flat, shoulders above hips and feet back (see figure 7.1).

As the front rows engage, lift your grounded knee and allow your shoulders to move forward firmly against the prop's rear thigh. Lock into your safe scrummaging position and push or resist on command. No matter how the scrum moves, keep your weight balanced within your stance. As the ball leaves the scrum, break off your bind and join in the next piece of action as quickly as possible.

Pushing and Locking-Out Techniques in the Scrum

Both are very similar. If you are to push, you extend your legs until they are just slightly bent at the knee. On a given signal by the forwards' leader, you extend your legs; if you are successful in moving your opponents backward, take short, sharp steps forward.

When your opponents push against you, direct all your effort downward into your hips and knees, lock the joints, but keep your shoulders above your hips at all times. This should stop you from going backward. The only point that may slide backward is your point of contact with the ground. If you only have three or four studs per boot in the ground, you may slide back quicker than if all were in contact. To make the best contact with the ground, you will have to turn your heels inward and downward until they touch the ground. If you have to take any steps backward, make them very short and brisk to try to regain a good stud hold.

If your opponents are to put the ball into the scrummage, you may decide to go for an eight-player shove. In this case your hooker also takes up a pushing position, and you and your second-row partner will be able to put all of your weight through both of your shoulders. The force in your push comes from your legs, abdomen and lower back. An eight-player shove is most effective if all the players push on a given signal by the leader of the forwards. If the opposition goes backward, you should take short, brisk steps forward to regain your scrummaging position as quickly as possible.

How to Execute the Jump at the Line-Out

For an effective jump at the line-out, begin with a wide, stable stance and your hands ready, palms facing the hooker. Always take up your starting position, even though the ball may be going to one of the other jumpers in your line-out. A signal for this will be called out by the forwards' leader. As the ball is thrown in you should jump up and slightly toward the line of touch, eyes on the ball at all times. As you jump, the hooker should throw the ball to the desired height, which is normally the highest point of your jump.

As you catch, bring the ball down quickly to your chest and turn your back toward your opponent's line. Your support players should by then have secured you and the ball, and you can release the ball to them. The same technique is used if you are to tap down the ball. A tap is simply a gentle touch with one or both hands, pushing the ball down to the scrum half. Follow the ball from the line-out or join in the resulting ruck or maul sequence.

Develop a range of jumps to beat your opponent. You will succeed only with clear and easily understood signals between you and the hooker. To practise all of your line-out skills, work with support players, one in front and one behind. Always jump in toward the line of touch, even when you have no opposition. Your support players can then also practise their skills.

It is a good idea to practise jumping against a tackle shield as you jump for the ball. Make sure the shield is held at your jump height so that you make shoulder contact with it. This will give you the confidence you need to jump against an opponent. You can then take the tackle shield away, but begin with passive opposition (your opponent jumps but does not try to go for the ball) and gradually progress to a competition for possession.

Table 7.1
Prop
Individual—Comfortable with contact. Has overall strength, but particularly in the shoulders, chest, back and legs.
Scrum—Provides a solid platform for the hooker to win the ball. *Loose-head:* Resists the force from opponents. *Tight-head:* Holds a strong, square position.
Line-out—Supports the jumper in the jump-and-catch sequence. Quickly closes off any gaps. Protects the ball. Sometimes acts as a sweeper, the player who gathers up any loose balls. Occasionally acts as a forward, peeling around the back of the line-out. *On opposition's throw:* Drives through any gaps and tries to win back ball.
Loose—Contributes to the attacking and defending sequences of the team. Stays on feet in contact. Maintains a good body position in rucks and mauls. Drives dynamically into contact. Moves quickly to support the ball carrier, particularly at kick-off.

(continued)

Table 7.1 *(continued)*

Hooker

Individual—Comfortable with contact. Flexible in shoulders, lower back and hips. Has overall strength, but particularly across shoulders.

Scrum—Wins own ball. Pressures opposition's.

Line-out—Throws accurately to the jumpers. Cleans up any spilled ball. *On opposition's throw:* Cleans up spilled ball. Sweeps around the front of the line-out and chases the ball.

Loose—Contributes to the attacking and defending sequences of the team. Stays on feet in contact. Maintains a good body position in rucks and mauls. Drives dynamically into contact. Runs in support of the ball carrier.

Lock

Individual—Has overall strength, but particularly in legs, buttocks, lower back and shoulders. Good ball handler, especially when jumping to catch at arm's length.

Scrum—Provides solid support for the front row. Exerts power forward when required. Resists the opposition's shove. Binds tightly throughout the scrum.

Line-out—Wins own ball. Competes vigorously against the opposition.

Loose—Catches the kick-off. Contributes to the team's attacking and defending sequences. Maintains a good body position in rucks and mauls. Drives dynamically into contact. Runs in support of the ball carrier.

FRONT FIVE SUCCESS STOPPERS

The following are common errors made by the Prop, Hooker and Lock. Have a trained instructor watch you for these problems.

Error	Correction
Prop	
1. When you are in the scrum, especially against live opposition, you seem to be very unstable.	1. Make sure that your coach checks your body position (see figure 7.1). If your position is safe and effective, check to make sure that your stance is wide enough (see diagram 7.1) and that your feet are slightly back from underneath your hips.
2. You never seem to be able to cope with the strength of the opposition's drive and constantly have to give ground slightly.	2. Make sure that you have as many studs in the ground as possible. Take as much of the drive force into your legs and hips as you can without becoming unstable: Use them like a spring that is compressed slightly. Move your feet backward only if you feel as though you are about to become unstable.
3. Each time the ball is thrown into your line-out, your jumper moves before you can react.	3. Know the signals for the throw. Watch the jumper with your head up. Take up a stance that allows you to read the hooker's throwing style. Move as soon as you recognise the throw, and put your hands to the jumper as soon as the jumper touches the ball.

Error	Correction
Hooker	
1. You throw inconsistently.	1. Practice is essential. Try throwing in one smooth movement from a starting point behind your head. This will help to prevent unnecessary ball movement in the throwing sequence. Holding the ball in two hands for as long as possible gives you more control over the accuracy of the throw.
2. When hooking, your legs do not seem long enough to reach the ball near the mouth of the tunnel.	2. This may be the fault of the scrum half. Ask for a much firmer delivery of the ball into the tunnel and you may find it easier to strike for. Pull your loose head closer, and move yourself nearer to the mouth of the tunnel.
3. Sometimes you are unable to strike because of the pressure from the opposition.	3. Sink your hips a little more into the scrummage and swivel your hips round slightly to face the mouth of the tunnel. Also work on your flexibility in the shoulders, lower back and hips.
Lock	
1. Any force you generate in the scrum never seems to be powerful enough to move it forward.	1. Check that you are bound tightly to your partner at lock and also to the prop. As the ball is put into the scrum, squeeze your arms, bend your legs, lower your knees and drive.
2. You have a tendency to slide backward when the opposition drives.	2. Make firm stud contact with the ground. The more studs you have in the surface, the better. This might mean that you have to turn your heels inward and downward when the pressure comes on. Accept some of the force into your knees and hips, like a spring being compressed, and then lock these joints out against any more backward movement. Move your feet only if you feel that you are becoming unstable.
3. You have a tendency to flap at the ball in the line-out, which gives an uncontrolled ball to your scrum half.	3. Ask the hooker to throw slightly lower and more softly. This will give you the chance to jump at the ball and drive your hands toward it. If you time your jump as well, you should be able to reach the ball before your opponent has the chance to contest it.
4. During each match your opponent eventually reads your signals or recognises how you intend to win the ball and begins to make it more difficult to gain possession.	4. Always practise a range of jumping techniques. This will keep your opponent guessing and should produce a better chance of winning a controlled ball.

FRONT FIVE

DRILLS

1. Body Position in the Scrum: Props

Most teams have an area designated for scrummaging, possibly with a machine to help you learn correct techniques. Include a hooker in your front row and begin practising as a front row against a machine.

To simulate the correct scrummaging position, always go to the left of the player opposite you. If you are a loose head, scrummage against one player; if you are a tight head, scrummage against two or against a machine.

Remember to bind tightly with a wide stance. Engage your opponent firmly, drive slightly upward, with your hips and shoulders square. Settle quickly, then keep movement to a minimum. Shoulders should always be above your hips. As soon as the ball is won, rejoin the support as quickly as possible.

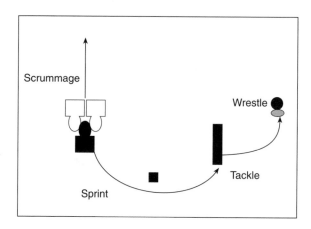

Success Goal = 10 consecutive firm nudges up and into opponent, keeping safe position ___

✔ *Success Check*

- Engage correctly: crouch, touch, pause, engage ___
- Keep head up, chin off chest, shoulders always above hips ___
- Drive shoulders slightly upward, hips slightly down ___
- If shoulders move forward or backward, take short steps to reposition ___

▃▅ *To Increase Difficulty*

- Scrummage against the machine or opponent(s), keeping a good position, and then sprint 10 metres to the left around a marker and back to scrummage again.
- Repeat preceding variation, but alternate sprinting to the left and to the right. Repeat 10 times each for 20 sprints.
- Sprint from scrum and rip a ball from another player's grasp.
- Between each scrum perform a simple sequence of movement (e.g., sprint, knock over a tackle bag, rip a ball from another player and return to the scrum). Repeat 10 times.

To Decrease Difficulty ▅▃

- After each scrummage, step back 3 or 4 metres, then engage again.

2. Binding and Engaging: Front Row

Practise binding and then engaging against the scrummage machine until you feel comfortable. It is then time to scrummage against three other players. It is essential that the players opposite you are used to playing in this position and know all safety factors and correct techniques.

Practise engaging so that you remain immediately stable. Then practise nudging the other group slightly upward and backward in the scrum. As you become more proficient, your opposition may apply a little more pressure of resistance so that you begin to develop some scrummaging strength as well as technique. If you feel the scrummage is in any way unstable, go back to the machine and determine the cause of instability with your coach.

Success Goal = 10 out of 10 stable scrums showing firm engagement, safe position and good technique ___

Success Check
- Feet flat and slightly more than shoulder-width apart ___
- Head up, chin off chest, back flat ___
- Shoulders always above hips, legs bent ___
- Crouch, touch, pause, engage ___

To Increase Difficulty
- Work against a number of different front rows in sequence.

To Decrease Difficulty
- Concentrate solely on technique.
- Concentrate on quality rather than quantity.

3. Binding, Engaging, Pushing and Locking Out: Front Five

The addition of two locks to the front row will give you a front five. Work against a scrummage machine so that you can practise pushing. Bind correctly and tightly before you go into the scrum. Locks should remember to put the majority of the push into the outside shoulder: The inside shoulder may have nothing to push against because the hooker may move independently of the props.

To lock out, you should practise pushing against the machine until your legs are almost straight and then stay in that position without moving for 5 seconds. You can do this only if you have a modern scrummage machine that has a number of strong elastic bands, which exert pressure back at you. If you do not have access to a machine, practise against five other players.

Follow up the scrummage with a series of activities to simulate subsequent play, for example, scrummage, sprint and handle, return to the scrum.

Success Goals =
a. 8 out of 10 successful attempts to move your opponents or scrummage machine backward ___
b. 8 out of 10 successful attempts to resist or slow down the opposition drive ___
c. 10 out of 10 successful, fast movements involving all front five away from scrum ___

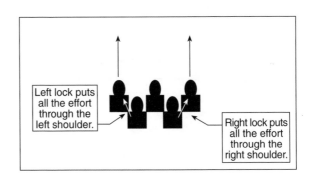

Left lock puts all the effort through the left shoulder.

Right lock puts all the effort through the right shoulder.

✔ Success Check

- Good scrummaging position ___
- To push forward, squeeze arms and grip, lower knees, straighten legs ___
- Short, brisk steps to regain position if opposition gives ground ___
- To resist a shove, lock hip and knee joint ___
- Heels in and down if necessary ___
- Best possible stud contact with ground ___

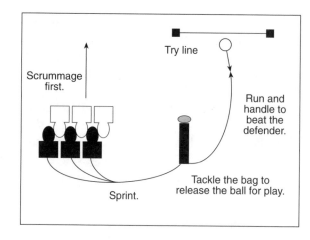

To Increase Difficulty

- Add more people to the opposition or more force to the scrummage machine.

To Decrease Difficulty

- Remove some of the weight of the opposition.

4. Hooking Practice: Front Row

Initially practise against a machine until your technique and timing improve. Practise the different ways of striking—you never know when you will need to use them. Work with the scrum half you normally play with so that you can become used to each other's signals.

While you are learning how to hook, the opposition front row should concentrate on supporting you as a hooker, so you can practise your technique without the pressure of an opponent trying to win the ball.

It is essential that all safety factors be applied in live scrummaging. Remember, shoulders always above hips. Avoid any mismatches in size, strength, weight or between props in opposition to each other or front rows as a unit.

⌒ Success Goals =

a. 10 successive successful strikes through the loose-head prop's feet ___

b. 10 successful strikes using two different hooking techniques ___

✔ Success Check

- Correct and tight binding at all times ___
- Shoulders parallel to ground ___
- Hips and head toward mouth of tunnel ___
- Use two most effective striking techniques ___

To Increase Difficulty

- Have someone drop a small object (e.g., a golf ball or coin) from directly above the strike area. Hook it as it hits the ground.
- Allow the opposition front row to be a little more active, for example, a slight nudge as the ball is put in. Note that 3 vs. 3 can become very unstable if your opponents narrow their stance and try to push. The nudge should come from the thighs and buttocks and should travel forward no more than 15 centimetres.
- Opposition hooker strikes as well. Props must maintain their wide stances to support both players.

To Decrease Difficulty

- Ask your scrum half to use a verbal signal to trigger the strike.
- Opponents remain passive, with no strike from the opposition hooker.

5. Live Scrummaging: Front Five Forwards Only

Practise against another unit of front five forwards who are of the same ability. Try to work with the scrum half who will be playing in the next game. You all have to be familiar with each other's styles of play and signals.

a. Decide whether you will be attacking or defending in the scrum. Line up, bind tightly, crouch and on the forward leaders' signal engage the opposition. Practise either your pushing and hooking or your locking-out techniques, but between each attempt break up and reform the scrum. Now is also the time to practise the all player push. In this practice sequence there are only five in the scrum, but in a game there will be three more and it is then called an "8 man drive". The hooker can take up a pushing position to contribute to the drive, and the locks can shove through both shoulders.

b. Run a 1-minute sequence that includes some of the skills you would normally have to perform in the game, for example, scrummaging, running, tackling, rucking or mauling and then back to scrummaging. Repeat five times.

Success Goals =

a. 10 firm, stable contacts with safe body positions and effective scrummaging skills ___

b. 10 firm, stable contacts, then quick movement to next action ___

Success Check

• Going forward: Sink knees and hips, straighten legs ___

• Resisting shove: Feet further back, knees and hips down, lock hip and knee joints ___

• If unbalanced, quickly regain position ___

To Increase Difficulty

• Scrummage in 5 different positions on the field. Between each scrum, run at pace while handling the ball.

• Alternate between pushing and locking.

To Decrease Difficulty

• Work for quality rather than quantity.

• Walk from one position to the next and concentrate solely on technique.

6. Live Scrummaging: Front Five Plus Back Row

Stability in the scrummage occurs only if the first contact is firm and strong from both teams. Much of the stability comes from the width of your stance. If your stance is narrow, the scrum will become very unstable as soon as any push comes on. The stabilising forces for the two locks are the flankers and number 8. The flankers will help to steady the prop forward platform and the number 8 will bind together the locks.

a. Line up facing the opposition, and crouch so that you can see where you will put your head. All players should look at the opposition. On the forwards' leader's signal, engage firmly, making sure that you do not recoil from the opposition and also stay balanced on making contact.

b. After each scrummage, play through a number of other sequences of action: For example, play a back row move which goes to a ruck, followed by further movement downfield until a stoppage occurs. Restart the game with a line-out and attack with the possession won until you score or the attack breaks down. Restart with another set piece.

Success Goals =

a. 10 firm, stable contacts with safe body positions and no backward or sideways movement ____
b. 10 firm, stable contacts, then arriving first at next action ____

✔ Success Check

- Firm, wide stance ____
- Shoulders always above hips, feet back ____
- Head up, chin off chest, lock in to opposition ____
- Firm binding with the player at the side of you and those in front ____
- No sideways movement ____

To Increase Difficulty

- Work against your opponents with very little rest between scrummages (but never until your strength begins to fail).

To Decrease Difficulty

- Work solely on technique, taking long rests between each scrum.

7. Practising Line-Out Skills: Front Five and Scrum Half

Use the 5- and 15-metre lines on the field for practising throwing over the distances used in a match. So that you can practice playing away from the line-out, use four other players to act as defenders. Place two close to the line-out to act as a back row defence and two others 10 metres back to simulate part of the mid-field defence. The thrower and jumpers work together, and the other props take their normal line-out positions. Props must react to each of the jumper's actions and provide support. The ball is then fed to the scrum half who runs either to the left or right and pops the ball back inside to a support runner. As a group you now have to attack the defence and try to score.

Success Goal = 8 out of 10 successful attacks with no dropped passes ____

✔ Success Check

- Props wedge the jumper as ball is caught ____
- Props quickly close on the jumper when tapping ____
- Good attacking decisions ____
- Running lines create spaces in defence ____
- Ball always turned back inside towards the centre of the grid when space becomes tight near the edge of it ____

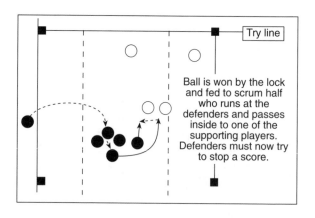

Ball is won by the lock and fed to scrum half who runs at the defenders and passes inside to one of the supporting players. Defenders must now try to stop a score.

To Increase Difficulty

- Allow the defenders to be very vigorous, but not to tackle.
- Keep the practise channel narrow.
- Move some of the marker cones inward so that the practise channel becomes gradually narrower as it nears the goal line.

To Decrease Difficulty

- Move some of the marker cones outward so that the practise channel gradually widens as it nears the goal line.
- Decrease the number of defenders.
- Before the throw, decide whether the jumper is to catch or tap.
- Scrum half signals intentions much earlier.

8. Supporting Receiver at Kick-Off: Props

Use an area about 10 metres wide by 25 metres long. The ball should be thrown over the distance you would expect it to be kicked. In this practice you should have one receiver, who is normally a lock and two supporters, the props and another player to act as scrum half. When practising your support techniques as a prop, you will need to stand close to the lock you will be playing with in the next game. As soon as the ball is thrown you should watch it as it flies and at the same time move in close to the catcher in order to offer some protection from your opponents by binding onto the receiver when he or she lands with the ball. Practise without any opponents initially and then extend the practice to include three chasers, who should try to prevent you from winning clean possession.

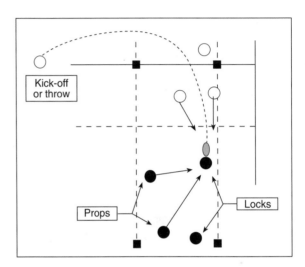

Success Goal = 5 out of 5 successful attempts at moving the ball through the practise channel to score a try, with minimum contact ___

Success Check
• Good body positions in contact ___
• Effective decisions ___
• Stability in contact ___
• Minimize contact situations ___
• Smooth, continuous movement ___

To Increase Difficulty
• Narrow the practise channel as it nears the goal line.
• Have the same number of defenders as attackers.

To Decrease Difficulty
• Decrease the number of defenders.
• Widen the practise channel as it nears the goal line.
• Give tackle pads to some of the defenders.

9. Accuracy at the Line-Out: Hooker

Your practice area should contain a range of targets, for example, lines on a wall, basketball rings and so on. Practise throwing at the targets, working around all of them to practise all your throws.

Success Goals =

a. Hit each target 5 times out of 10 ____

b. Hit a series of different targets 5 times out of 10 ____

Success Check

• Correct distance from target ____
• Ball in 2 hands above head ____
• Throw with arms and upper body, both hands on ball as long as possible ____
• Throw to desired height ____

To Increase Difficulty

• Make three throws, then follow with a sequence of work: For example, sprint, tackle a tackle bag, grapple for the ball with an opponent, then return for another three throws.

To Decrease Difficulty

• Make the target areas bigger.

10. Winning the Ball: Locks

To practise jumping to win the ball at the line-out while working against opposition you will also need a scrum half to give the ball to. First practise against a player holding a tackle shield, but as soon as possible work against an unshielded player so that you become used to jumping for the ball and making shoulder-to-shoulder contact.

Success Goal = Clean possession from 5 throws, using effective signals ____

Success Check

• Inside foot forward, weight on back foot ____
• On signal, jump to line of touch ____
• Catch, tap with 2 hands or guide with 1 hand to win ball ____

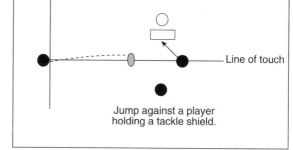

Jump against a player holding a tackle shield.

To Increase Difficulty

• Opposition becomes more active until full competition takes place.

To Decrease Difficulty

• Slow down the introduction of active opposition.

11. Throwing to the Jumpers: Hooker

Once you have the accuracy and your jumpers are confident, you should try out your throws in a full practice situation. It is essential that your opposition does not know your line-out signals. Start out with opposition only against each jumper, and gradually progress to a fully opposed line-out. After each throw try to score over your opponent's goal line. When you return to the line-out to restart the practice keep moving it to different points up and down the touch line so that you also have to practise reforming the line. It's important to practise throwing to different lengths and following the ball into the play to tidy up any possessions.

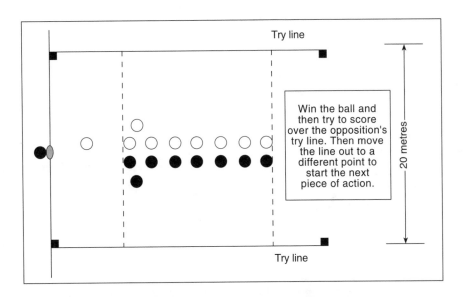

Win the ball and then try to score over the opposition's try line. Then move the line out to a different point to start the next piece of action.

Success Goals =
a. 7 out of 10 accurate throws to jumper ___
b. 10 out of 10 throws to correct signalled position ___

Success Check
- Spread fingers across seams ___
- Both hands on ball as long as possible ___
- Follow ball onto field ___
- Clean up balls that are knocked down near front ___
- React immediately to uncaught balls ___

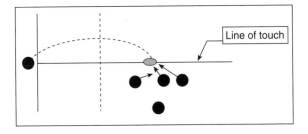

To Increase Difficulty
- Work through 10 line-outs calling the signal immediately as the line-out is formed and play through the sequence reforming the line-outs without rest or pause.
- After each throw, follow with a sequence of activity: For example, catch and drive the ball, to develop passing among the forwards, return and throw again.
- With full opposition, work between 2 lines 10 metres apart; both sets of forwards try to win the ball and score over the goal line.

To Decrease Difficulty
- Work for quality rather than quantity.
- The opposition stays very passive.
- Use a slightly smaller ball so that you can grip it better.
- With passive line-out opposition, work from a line of touch 10 metres from the goal line, win the ball and then try to score against an active defence.

12. Game Sequences: Front Five

Practise line-outs as part of a game. This could be any type of game, for example, touch and pass, tag rugby, end ball or a practice match. The line-out starts the sequence of action each time. You could, for example, substitute a line-out for a scrum when playing touch and pass. You might play a 10 vs. 10 game of touch rugby with backs playing against forwards. You can make up games from your own experience as long as some of the essential elements of the game of rugby remain in the practise. For example: Pass backwards, release the ball after a "tackle" (this may be a two-handed touch at the waist), play line-outs when the ball goes off the side of the field, after a technical infringement (knock-on, forward pass, etc.) bring the ball back into play using a scrum, free kick to simulate a set piece situation. If a back mishandles, start the game with a line-out.

Success Goal = 8 clean possessions out of 10 throws in a game ___

Success Check
• Clear signals between thrower and jumper ___
• Correct foot positioning ___
• Hands above shoulders, fingers spread ___
• Jump inward to land at line of touch ___

To Increase Difficulty
• Work against another group of forwards.
• Develop the opposition from relatively passive to fully active.

To Decrease Difficulty
• Opposition cannot contest the ball.

FRONT FIVE SUCCESS SUMMARY

Success is measured in the amount of possession you win and protect in the game. Whether from the scrum, line-out or kick-off, your role in the front five is to win the ball so that others can use it. If you are also skilful enough to become part of the attacking sequences in the game then so much the better. The best front five players are also able to set up and continue running and handling sequences which lead to tries. As you practise the previous drills, focus on perfecting your support and ball-winning skills and you will become a valuable asset to your team.

STEP 8

THE MIDDLE FIVE: THE USERS

The players who occupy the middle five positions are the back row (blind-side flanker, open-side flanker and number 8) and the two half backs (scrum half and fly half). These players are the primary users of the ball. It is they who work hard to set up attacks for the rest of the team. They pin down the defence and create space for others. They are also the main unit who act as link players between the front and back five players. They are also a major defensive unit in the team and are often the players who make the first defensive tackles against an attack from a set piece.

The Back Row: Flankers and Number 8

Teams that have a good back row are normally very successful. Although the players work as a tight unit in attack and defence, the positions have slightly different skills. All the back-row players need speed and contact skills, especially in the tackle. The open-side flanker should also possess a range of attacking skills, similar to those of the centres, to add to the continuity skills of the team.

Good back-row players are often interchangeable, for example, an open-side flanker might play in the number 8 position at a scrum when the back row initiates an attack by picking up the ball at the base of the scrum and running at the defence. This should only happen when the ball-carrying back-row forward has particularly good attacking skills or has the power to drive through close contact situations (see diagram 8.1). This kind of flexibility within this small unit will make the best use of all three players. By interchanging, they may become most creative in attack and most destructive in defence. This will make best use of each of the players in the back row and is different to the traditional configuration as shown in

Figure 8.1. All back-row players need well-developed contact and continuity skills.

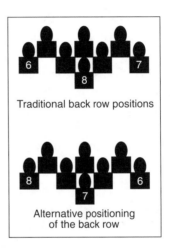

Diagram 8.1 Open-side flanker as number 8.

Positional Requirements

These are the main priorities of the flankers and number 8:

At the Scrum

- Push (see figure 8.1).
- Defend, or support or initiate an attack.
- Number 8 controls the ball at the base of the scrum and when necessary initiates attacks from this position.

In the Line-Out

- If you are tall, you can become an extra jumper in the line.
- As part of the defence from the line-out, tackle any players who attack close or cover across the field to defend against an attack out wide.

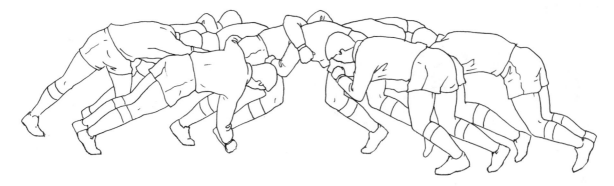

Figure 8.1 No. 8 attacks from the base of the scrum.

- Move quickly to a position that allows you to either defend or support close in or near the mid-field.
- When required, act as a sweeper or support peels off the end of the line-out go forward.

In the Loose

- Approach all rucks and mauls vigorously.
- Drive in dynamically at rucks and mauls with good body position.
- Understand when to join rucks and mauls and when to stay out, as determined by attacking options and defensive requirements.
- Rip the ball out of rucks and mauls.
- Support all attacks and act as the dynamo who fires up the rest of the team.
- Make more tackles than any other player.

Your role as a back-row player is to make best use of any ball you manage to scavenge in the game. You may win this ball in very close contact situations or in the open field. Your choice of follow-up attack may be to maintain the continuity by passing to someone in a better position or to take on a defender who is blocking your team's progress up the field. Your decision is crucial to the continuity of the attack.

As a general rule it is far better to pass the ball into the space at the side of a defender rather than make contact. More often than not, passing guarantees continuity in attack, whereas contact does not, unless your players have particularly good continuity skills. For a review of footwork skills for avoiding contact, see Step 3.

Although you should try to avoid as many collisions as possible, you need to practise continuity in contact. No matter how good a player you are, there will be times when you will be caught by the opposition with the ball. As the ball carrier, you have a range of options if you are about to make contact with an opponent. For a review of contact situations, see Step 6.

Scrum Half

The scrum half is one of the most important positions on the team. The scrum half is the link between the forwards and the backs and is the pivot around which the majority of attacks take place. You will be called on throughout the game to make instant decisions in attack and defence. In the game you have three simple decisions to make: Will you kick, pass or run? The quality of your decision will determine the quality of your team's performance.

You are the major decision maker in the team: at line-out you may give the signal for the throw; at the scrum you may call the back-row moves; at rucks and mauls you may choose which side to attack. You must communicate all these decisions, so more than anyone else, you should be constantly talking to the forwards and backs.

You are also in the best place and may be the ideal player to act as pack leader for the team. You should play with your head up, looking for weaknesses in the defence to be better able to decide whether your forwards should drive the ball through contact, release it or drive in contact so that a player with the ball can drive out from the side of the maul to set up the next attack. You become the eyes and ears of the players in the pack.

If you are to develop as a scrum half, you should practise passing from the ground to the left and right.

You have an advantage if you are left handed because the vast majority of passes from the base of the scrum are made with the left hand. This becomes more important as you begin to play in adult rugby, because under the laws which govern adult rugby, the opposition scrum half can follow you round and stand next to your team's number 8, thereby cutting off any right-hand pass.

Positional Requirements

These are the main priorities of the scrum half:

At the Scrum

- Pass accurately to both left and right without lift or back swing.
- Pivot round on your back foot to protect the pass (pivot pass). Use a pivot pass when necessary.
- Pose a constant threat to the defence.
- Kick accurately with your right foot for position.
- Be the first tackler when the opposition uses a back-row attack down their left side of the scrum.

At the Line-Out

- Pass accurately and quickly to either left or right, no matter how the ball arrives to you.
- Kick accurately with either foot for position.

In the Loose

- Pass accurately to either side.
- Kick accurately.
- Pose a constant threat to the defence.
- Contribute to the defence around rucks and mauls.

Passing Skills

There are a number of different passes which a scrum half should master especially from the base of the scrum. The ball receiver may be running at speed close by or fading away from the pass some 10 metres away. You must therefore not think the only pass a scrum half should deliver is one that spirals out point first over a great distance. A problem with the spiralling motion is that it creates a great deal of force, which can push your fly half sideways to control the ball. This forces the rest of the backs also to run diagonally (see diagram 8.2).

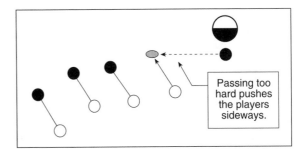

Passing too hard pushes the players sideways.

Diagram 8.2 Result of passing too hard.

The scrum half's pass must be delivered so it gives the three-quarter line a range of options. Too hard and it may force them sideways, too soft and it may check their forward movement. You should therefore try to develop the following range of passes (see diagram 8.3):

1. A pass that spirals point first and covers a long distance so that your fly half can play around the edge of the back-row defence.
2. A spiral pass that travels belly first. This arrives at the fly half over a shorter distance, does not fly as quickly and is much easier to control. This will allow the fly half to play closer to the back-row defence and put someone else around the edge of it.
3. Finally, passes that do not spin at all and are used to bring forwards or backs onto the ball at pace, often very close to the opposition. These passes are flicked or popped up using just the fingers, wrists and forearms and may turn gently end over end.

How to Execute the Pass From the Scrum

The best way to describe the action for moving the ball quickly off the ground is a brushing motion. Try

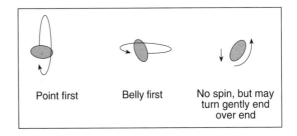

Point first   Belly first   No spin, but may turn gently end over end

Diagram 8.3 Passing variation 3.

to imagine there is some dust on the grass and just brush your hand across the surface of the grass to move the dust away. If you now make the brushing motion much longer and more vigorous so that your hand starts near your back foot and finishes up and beyond the opposite shoulder, you will be making the passing movement.

You will find passing from the ground much easier if you take a wide stance with legs slightly bent and weight toward your back foot. Practise the motion without the ball at first. As your arm moves through its arc, allow your weight to follow it so that it finishes over the other foot. This transfer of weight helps you put power into the pass. Pointing your front foot in the direction of the pass also helps you to shift your weight from the back to the front foot. Always start from a standing position, and make the imaginary pass in one movement: Stride in the direction of the pass, bend the knees, sink the hips, reach down, sweep away and point along the path of the ball.

Once this feels smooth, practise the pass sequence with the ball. Place the ball on the ground so that it is already pointing in the passing direction. To pass to your right, step into the ball with your left foot first, and then plant and point your right foot towards the target receiver. To pass to the left do everything as a mirror image.

Initially you should use only one hand to move the ball away (see figure 8.2). To pass to the left, use your right hand. Reach down with your passing hand behind the ball, spread your fingers wide near the back of the ball, and sweep away to the receiver. Make sure your hand follows through so that it points in the direction of the pass. (It may take you a number of attempts before you manage to make the ball fly off the ground.) To make the ball spin, bring your hand up the side of the ball as you pass it. Practise more with your non-dominant hand so that passes from either side are of the same quality.

After successfully sweeping the ball away with one hand, it is time to use both hands. Approach the ball while keeping low to the ground. Watch the ball at all times, hands ready as a target. Step into the ball quickly, pointing the leading foot at the receiver (see figure 8.3a). Your rear hand sweeps the ball away in one movement while the front hand acts solely as a guide (see figure 8.3b). Do not be tempted to put your guide hand fully on the ball. Begin by touching it only with the tip of your index finger and thumb (see figure 8.3d). This will prevent you from picking up the ball before you pass it. Finish low with hands pointing at the receiver.

When you wish to spin the ball point first, simply bring the fingers of your back hand from the rear base of the ball, up the side to over the top of it as you move from your rear to leading foot. If you wish to spin the ball belly first, spread your fingers wide and put them down at right angles to the seam. As you sweep the ball to release it, the belly of the ball rather than the point will be heading toward the receiver. Again, simply bring the fingers of your back hand from the bottom of the ball up the side and over the top to make it spin.

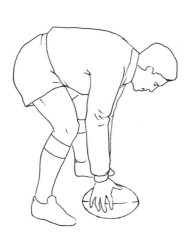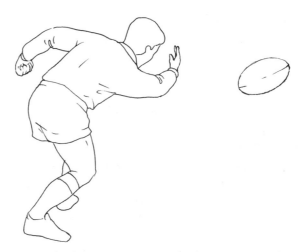

Figure 8.2 Sweep ball away with one hand.

FIGURE
8.3 **KEYS TO SUCCESS**

PASSING FROM THE SCRUM

Preparation

1. Keep low to ground ___
2. Watch ball, hands ready as target ___

Execution

1. Step to ball quickly, point leading foot at the receiver ___
2. Rear hand sweeps ball away in one movement ___
3. Front hand only guides ___

Follow-Through

1. Finish low with hands pointing at receiver ___
2. Rejoin game immediately ___

The scrum half must select a pass to suit the attacking or defensive situation. The position of the receiver will decide the length of pass as you approach the ball. Passing too fast and hard or too soft and slow will be detrimental to the performance of your team. If a long pass is demanded, you should send out a fast, spinning, point-first pass. If a short pass is required, send out a belly-first pass. As soon as you feel confident, you should play against a defender who arrives either wide or close. It is the receiver's decision whether to try to run outside the defender or become the target of the defender's tackle and pass to an overlapping player. A spare player can roll the ball to you so that you can begin to practise under match-like conditions.

There are occasions when the scrum half has to deliver a very short, soft pass from the ground to a player running at pace. A spiral pass is not appropriate in this situation. The scrum half should develop a soft or flick pass that can travel from half a metre to 5 metres. This pass can be made from any point within your stance. and often it will be passed from outside your base. All the effort comes from the wrists and fingers. When you reach the limit distance of such a pass, you may also bring your forearms into play, which give some extra length to your pass. As you pick up the ball, keep your fingers spread wide around it and simply flick your wrists and fingers in the direction you wish the pass to travel. If your fingers are pointing downward, flick them in an upward movement; if your fingers are pointing directly forward, flick them sideways. Avoid spinning the ball for such a pass.

How to Execute a Kick From the Scrum

The scrum half is an ideal player to kick the ball because the forwards often provide a shield against the opposition. Although it helps if you are left handed for passing, it's better if you are right footed for kicking, because a kick over the top of the scrum can be effectively achieved only with your right foot. If you try to kick with your left, the opposition scrum half will be able to charge it down. Kicking from the base of the scrum is a simple skill, but players often have difficulty with it because they may take too many paces from picking up the ball to kicking.

To kick effectively you should take up a position behind the ball at the base of the scrum, plant your right foot slightly to the right of the ball and your left foot close to it, simply scoop up the ball in both hands, then stride across with your left foot (see diagram 8. 4 and figure 8.4a). The point and seams of the ball should point in the direction it is to be kicked. As you start your kick, transfer the ball to the palm of your right hand and drop it onto your right foot (see figure 8.4, b-c). Watch the ball down onto your foot, and kick high and through the ball (see figure 8.4d). In simple words the sequence is "plant, scoop, step, kick".

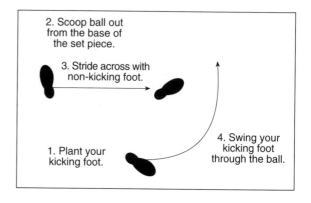

Diagram 8.4 Plant, scoop, stride and kick.

FIGURE
8.4 **KEYS TO SUCCESS**

KICKING FROM THE SCRUM

a   b   c   d

Preparation

1. Wide stance, eyes on ball ____
2. Hands ready to scoop ball from scrum ____

Execution

1. Scoop ball away ____
2. Step to side with non-kicking foot ____
3. Ball in palm ____
4. Kick up and through ball ____

Follow-Through

1. Foot follows through high ____
2. Watch ball as it flies ____
3. Chase the ball to try and regain possession ____

There are two reasons for kicking over the top of a scrum. One is to gain ground: the ball rolls a long way downfield and eventually finds its way into touch; the other is to try to gain yardage and regain possession. The only way your side will be able to regain possession is if the ball is kicked high enough for them to arrive as it lands. It should also travel far enough toward your opponent's goal line to clear any danger for your side. The distance you aim for depends entirely on the speed of those who are chasing. You also have to take into account the height you can kick the ball. A ball that is in the air for a long time and goes forward the optimum distance gives more players the opportunity to arrive as it lands to contest possession.

You will also have opportunities to kick with your left foot, so you should give equal practice to both feet. If you find that one foot is much weaker than the other, you should concentrate on improving your kicking on that side.

There may be occasions when you have to use your foot near the touch line, which will reduce your angle to the touch line for the kick. If you have enough forwards in front of you, and they are providing a shield against a member of the opposition charging down your kick, it is far better to use the right foot near the left touch line, and the left foot near the right touch line.

If you are kicking to put the ball into touch, you should place your kicking foot farther back than before. Then pivot and stride with your other foot to bring your hips more round to face the touch line. This will allow you to kick the ball at an angle toward the side of the field so that it reaches touch.

There are times when you may not be the best person to kick to touch. If you are very close to the touch line, it may be better to give the ball to your fly half in order to widen the angle toward the touch line so that there is a better chance of achieving a greater distance. You must decide whether or not you have a good angle.

Running From the Scrum Half Position

Although you may be one of the players involved in an attack initiated by the back row, there are other occasions when you may seize the opportunity to run with the ball. Sometimes the ball may be delivered very quickly from good forward-driving play that releases you in behind the defence. At other times, the blind side may have very few defenders, and you can see an opportunity to attack with other members of your team. In both cases you must explode into top speed within two or three strides to take the defence by surprise. At the same time, lower your centre of gravity so that you can bounce off any would-be tacklers. At all times, you should try to carry the ball in two hands so that you can pass the ball away should you be confronted by a number of defenders. You should bring the ball onto your forearm only when there is space ahead of you.

When you practise running from the attack point, try to imagine situations that may confront you. A tackler may come from the left or from the right. In both cases you should be able to swerve one way or the other. You may have to dart suddenly from an outside to an inside running line so you should try to develop your sidestep (see Step 3).

A simple way to practise your running lines is to put markers down where the defenders would be if you ran from behind the scrum. As soon as you have rehearsed the runs then begin to replace the defender marker with a player who tries to tag you as you run.

You might now use some teammates as support runners. Your right winger and full back can be very potent attacking players from the scrum on the right-hand side of the field. Have them join you in your run, and play against two or three defenders.

Fly Half

The fly half is perhaps the most crucial player in the whole team. Teams that are lucky enough to have a fly half with vision, skill and understanding are of-

ten highly successful and very difficult to beat. To be a really good fly half you need to be a very calm, clear-thinking and skilful player. Your job is to find the best way to bring your attacking players, whether the wingers and full back or the back row, into the game.

Throughout the game the opposition will be attempting to pressure you in the hope that you will kick the ball aimlessly either up field or into touch. If you fall into such a trap, you end up giving the ball to your opponents. Therefore, you sometimes have to attack the opposition yourself to make some space for your back row or inside centre to drive in and support your strike at the defence.

The closer you can successfully play to the defence, the better. You must realise, however, that if you play close, the teammate two passes away may also be very close to them. If your pass is not accurate enough for such a style of play, your attacks will break down. To play successfully very close to the opposition, you must have excellent handling skills and be prepared to take on tacklers. This means that you sometimes must take some form of contact.

The alignment of your outer players (your centres) must constantly change to accommodate what you are trying to achieve in each attack. If they are too flat (not far enough behind you), they add no options to the attack (see diagram 8.5). It is far better if both your centres run so that they can read the number on your back. If your centres stay in good alignment, you will always have two passes available to you along

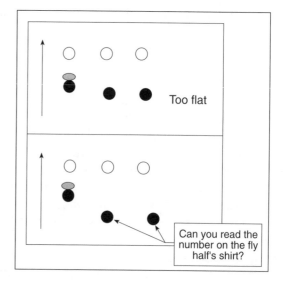

Too flat

Can you read the number on the fly half's shirt?

Diagram 8.5 Keep your depth.

the line, one to the inside centre and one to the outside centre. The patterns you and your centres play will constantly alter the width, depth and speed of your attacking runs. Remember, it is not where you are when you start your run that alters the shape of the defence, it is where you are in relation to the defence when you receive the ball. For example, close to the defence it is better to play a switch pass, whereas you should be farther away to play a loop.

Kicking Skills

It is not always possible or desirable to run with every ball you receive during the match. Sometimes you may have to kick the ball downfield. You can use a number of different types of kicks as attacking ploys, including the bomb, grubber, chip and wipers kick. Kicks are used to gain ground, regather possession or for position. See Step 5 for hints on how to kick effectively.

Kicking as an attacking ploy should be viewed primarily as a last resort after you have tried all your other attacking ploys. It may, however, be used to put the defence in two minds. If they are coming up very quickly, you might pop the ball in behind them. The next time they move out of defence, they may slow down their advance, which gives you time and space to close in on them at speed.

In order to kick for possession, you need to kick the ball high enough and far enough forward for your players to arrive under the ball as it lands (see diagram 8.6). Defenders and attackers will have to compete for the ball and so will have to jump in order to collect it.

There are two main requirements for kicks for possession:

1. Accuracy (attaining the proper height and distance with your kick)
2. Signals (calling so that people know you are going to kick)

Your scrum half is very likely to make a kick for possession to the right side of the field, because most scrum halves are right footed and it is an easy kick to make when the forwards are in front and can be used as a screen to prevent any charge down by the opposition. If you are also right footed, it is better for you to kick from the left side of the field, which gives you a wider angle, especially when kicking down the 15-metre line or high and toward the posts.

Any kicks that are to land in between the 22m and goal line must be accurate. If they are not accurate, the ball can be marked by the defending player catching the kick. Therefore you need a number of chasers who aim to arrive as the ball lands in order to contest the kick and prevent the mark. It is often better to kick high, so that the ball lands just outside the 22-metre area, because the catcher has to follow up with another action (run, pass or kick back). Whichever of these actions follows the kick, your team has the opportunity to regain possession and counter-attack.

You must practise your kicking regularly against some form of defence. Most players can kick the ball without the pressure of a defender. Only good players can kick accurately when someone is bearing down on them with the intention of charging down

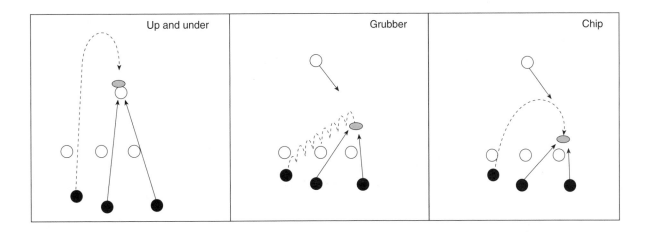

Diagram 8.6 Kicking in attack.

the kick. As fly half, you set the attacking tone of the team. You have to quickly assess the possibilities for attack, taking into account your position on the field, the quality of the possession, the closeness of the forwards and their ability to support the attack.

Passing Skills

Although there may be times in a game, especially from set pieces, when you organise a move to try to disrupt the defence, there are other times when you simply have to play without a plan. If the other players in the backs (particularly the back three—wingers and full back) understand their roles, they will run at gaps to attract defenders. Sometimes they will receive the ball from you if you notice that the gap has stayed open, and at other times they will act as decoys while you pass the ball across them to another teammate running into a gap. Good fly halves make instant decisions and can send out accurate passes to their support players.

It is very easy to deliver a pass without opposition, so you must work against a defender as soon as you feel capable. Your role in the game is to draw at least one defender toward you before you give the ball to your backs. You may sometimes hold the ball for four or five strides and other times move the ball as soon as you receive it.

The distance from the defence at which you release the ball depends on the point along the tackle line you are trying to reach. For example, if your attack is trying to go around the defence, you may need to make a long pass to cut out one of the usual receivers. You make this pass back from the defence so that it creates time and space for the outside players. If you are attacking close to the forwards, you carry the ball fast at the defence and attempt to pass to someone running into a gap.

There must be constant communication between all players on a rugby field. Sometimes the people running at gaps will call for the ball, and you should be able to make the pass required to put that player into space. At other times, you may realise that the defence is already at a disadvantage, and you will have to communicate this to the players outside you before or as you receive the ball. Rugby is not a telepathic exercise—communication speeds up the attack so that the defence finds it difficult to cope.

Table 8.1

Back row

Individual—Comfortable with contact. Has good handling ability. A good tackler. Fit enough to run at pace all through the game.

Scrum—Pushes in every scrum. Provides the first line of defence down the right side of the scrum, second tackler after the scrum half down the left hand side.

Line-out—Supports the jumper in jump-and-catch sequence. Quickly closes off any gaps. Protects the ball. Sometimes cleans up loose balls. Occasionally acts as a forward, peeling around the front of the line-out. *On opposition's throw:* Drives through any gaps and tries to win back ball. *Open-side flanker:* Threatens the first ball carriers in their backs. *Blind-side flanker:* Follows up and supports open-side, retrieves loose ball or tackles other ball carriers.

Loose—Contributes to team's attacking and defending sequences. Stays on feet in contact. Maintains a good body position in rucks and mauls. Drives dynamically into contact. Moves quickly to support the ball carrier in attack. Tackles the ball carrier in defence.

Scrum half

Individual—Quick in thought and action. Passes and kicks accurately and with precision. Strong legs and shoulders. Comfortable with contact against much bigger players. Decisive player who understands the game. Has the pace, power and endurance to work rate throughout the game.

Scrum—Passes cleanly off the ground under pressure. Kicks accurately over the scrum. Recognises attacking opportunities, particularly down right side. Takes part in defensive screen around the scrum.

Line-out—Handles the ball well when delivered from a range of heights and distances. Kicks accurately over the line-out. Passes under pressure from opposition hooker. Quickly covers the field in defence.

Loose—Tackles aggressively. Performs all skills under pressure. Creates space for others to use. Re-enters play quickly after contributing to attack or defence. Recognises gaps and the pace to go through them.

(continued)

Table 8.1 *(continued)*

Fly half

Individual—Quick in thought and action. Passes and kicks accurately and with precision. Decisive player who understands the game.

Scrum—Knows when to play flat or deep. Can stop the first defender with an effective running line. Takes part in defensive screen around the scrum.

Line-out—Plays close to the defence when needed. Kicks accurately under pressure. Can stop the opposition drift defence. Threatens the opposition. Creates space for others.

Loose—Constantly threatens the opposition. Handles and kicks with accuracy. Quickly identifies weaknesses in the opposition defence and takes best advantage of them.

FLANKERS AND NUMBER 8 SUCCESS STOPPERS

Error	Correction
1. You cannot produce the ball in contact situations.	1. Turn in to the tackle earlier than you would normally. This will prevent you from burying the ball into the defence and making it difficult to dig out. It will also keep the ball visible to the rest of your support.
2. The ball is released slowly after a contact situation.	2. Pass before you make contact, preferably into a space. If you have to make contact, stay strong on a wide base and keep the ball visible to your support.
3. The attack lacks continuity even though the ball is available.	3. Take the shortest route to the ball carrier: a straight line. Run at the nearest shoulder of any ball carrier, always expect a pass, but be ready to drive in to take the ball if the player makes contact with the opposition.
4. The opposition always seem to have a hand on the ball in contact situations.	4. If you drive in with the ball leading with your right shoulder, the next player must come in left shoulder first and drive up and into your chest. This will shut off the ball from the opposition.
5. Any back-row moves are stifled near the scrum.	5. Run your moves wider out from the side of the scrum, perhaps using the scrum half or full back as the first pass receiver. They will have more momentum because they will already be running when they receive the pass and therefore have a better chance of succeeding.

SCRUM HALF SUCCESS STOPPERS

Error	Correction
1. The pass wobbles rather than spirals.	1. Make sure that your hand is at right angles to the seam, and bring it up and over the top of the ball as you pass it. Spread the fingers of your rear hand and only touch lightly with those of your front hand.
2. There is no power in your pass.	2. Pass the ball from your rear foot, sweeping it through a long arc and transferring your weight from rear to front foot as you complete the pass.
3. You try to kick over the forwards but are constantly charged down.	3. Take only one stride from the base of the scrum and into the kick. Make sure that this stride is back away from the scrum to give you time and space to get the kick away.
4. The accuracy of the kick is not good.	4. Watch your foot to the ball. Turn your body sideways to the target area, gradually altering this angle until you have the ball flying in the correct direction. You can then work on the height.
5. You never seem to make a clean break from the base of the scrum.	5. Practise without opposition: Run your line around and swerve past a range of markers where the tacklers would be. Then add some of the tacklers, and practise your run to make sure that you have the correct line. Practise your running drills, especially those for explosive starts from standing.

FLY HALF SUCCESS STOPPERS

Error	Correction
1. The backs' moves are ineffective because the opposition are across the field awaiting the strike runner.	1. You are playing the game too far back from the defence, which allows them to drift across the field.
2. The outside backs seem to overrun the play.	2. Start a little deeper on the fly half, and time the runs from when the fly half sets up the pass.
3. The inside centre continuously drops the ball.	3. Make sure that you are not passing the ball too hard and directly at the player. Passes should be floated into a space in front of the receiver.

Error	Correction
4. All kicks are inaccurate.	4. Keep your head down and concentrate on striking through the centre of the ball. Also alter the angle of your hips to the target area to see if this helps.
5. The kicks go into touch very close to the kicking point.	5. To achieve the best distance, you should widen your angle if you can and kick left foot to right touch line and right foot to left touch line.

MIDDLE FIVE

DRILLS

1. Pass or Contact: Back Row

In this drill you must decide whether to pass or go into contact. If you go into contact, you must then decide how you will maintain the continuity of the attack. Do not pre-judge what the defender may do. If you can, pass; if not, make the bump and in a split second follow up this action with the nearest support player. Be decisive, be strong and work briskly.

In a grid measuring 20 metres by 15 metres, play 5 vs. 5, one side trying to score by avoiding contact if possible. At times, however, you will run out of useful space, and your only alternative will be to go to contact in order to take away one or two players from the defence. Your next decision is vital: move the ball early or keep driving forward?

Success Goal = 5 scores with continuous forward movement and without losing possession ___

Success Check
- Stable, wide bases in contact ___
- Keep ball moving forward ___
- Weight behind leading foot at point of contact ___
- Good driving body positions by support players ___

To Increase Difficulty
- Decrease the distance between defenders.
- Narrow the grid toward the goal line.
- Allow defenders to re-enter play toward the goal line after being passed.

To Decrease Difficulty
- Defenders stay only on their line and can only move side to side.
- Widen the grid as it approaches the goal line.

2. Working Through Contact: Back Row

Practise making contact 2 vs. 1. Imagine that there is no space to pass into and that you have to take a defender away from the area to give your support player a clear run upfield. Work in a narrow channel so that your support player has to stay close to you: 5 metres by 10 metres will be sufficient.

Success Goal = No dropped passes in 5 attempts ___

Success Check

- As you approach contact, lower centre of gravity ___
- Make long, slow, last stride into contact ___
- Drive low to high ___
- Sometimes pivot on front foot ___
- Gut pass: Push ball up to partner's lower chest ___

To Increase Difficulty

- Add one extra defender to the practice so that the ball carrier has the option to pass as well as run in order to beat the defence.
- Add more defenders down the channel for a continuous bump-and-pass sequence.

To Decrease Difficulty

- Allow the defenders to hold tackle shields.
- Add an extra attacker to support the first-pass receiver.

3. Running Lines: Back Row

Once you have practised running skills, you should try them in a game-like drill. To simulate a game, do not organise running lines or plan the contact area. Play spontaneously so that you can react accordingly. You and a flank-forward partner begin the practice by bumping into a defender, driving the ball forward and then feeding the ball to the scrum half. This ball goes two passes out either left or right, and you follow as you would in the game.

The second pass receiver runs at the defender and passes back inside to you very close to the defence. Your options will depend on your distance from the defender and on the closeness of your support. If you are a well-balanced runner with good handling skills, you may be able to catch and pass in a split second. If not, you may have to bump into the defender and find a way of keeping the ball alive. Will you spin out of contact and pass? bump and pass? bump and drive through? bump, spin and drive? The decision is yours. Your priority is to keep the ball moving at pace through the channel.

Success Goal = 5 out of 5 successful tries with no dropped balls ___

Success Check

- Decisive action at point of contact ___
- Wide base in contact ___
- Good driving positions ___
- Hands ready for all situations ___

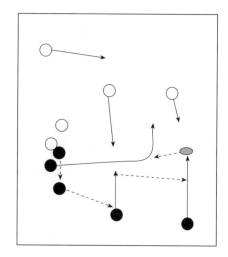

To Increase Difficulty
- Allow defenders to be very active.
- Allow second-pass receiver to take the ball into contact or pass inside.

To Decrease Difficulty
- Declare which technique to practise and set up the contact situation accordingly.

4. Pass and Contact Options: Back Row

Begin this practice as though you were about to initiate an attack from the scrum. You have two options in a back-row attack from a scrummage. You can either stay close to the scrum and make deliberate contact with the opposition back row, or you can stay close to the scrum and pass to someone else in a better position slightly farther out.

Decide which of the options you will take, pick up the ball and drive forward into the grid. If you have decided to make contact with your opponent, you must lead in with your right shoulder, take a long, low, last stride and bump up and into the tackler while pivoting around on your front foot so that the nearest player can see the ball.

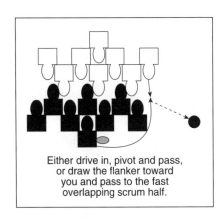

Either drive in, pivot and pass, or draw the flanker toward you and pass to the fast overlapping scrum half.

If, on the other hand, you are to set up a much faster attack 2 or 3 metres farther out, you need to have established a signal which will be given by your scrum half, so that the scrum half can leave the responsibility for the ball to you and can quickly run into the wider channel. The scrum half taps you on the hip and begins to run. As soon as you receive this signal you pick up the ball, drive round the right side of the scrum close in, draw the left-hand defending flanker toward you and make a pass to the fast-overlapping scrum half.

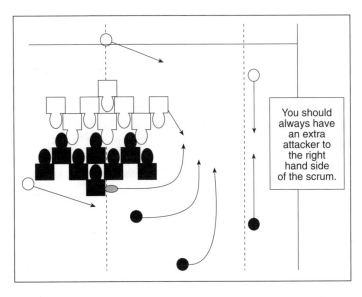

You should always have an extra attacker to the right hand side of the scrum.

If the opposition defence is well organised and has the same number of players to your back row, attacking the channel close in can often be a futile exercise. If you are quick and agile, the wider channel is the one for you, especially if one of the backs can release you or your back-row players onto the opposition defence.

One of the best places from which to play back-row attacks is the right side of the field, with a minimum of 15 metres between the scrum and the touch line. This will always allow you to have one extra player in the attack.

Use an 8-player scrum plus a scrum half, right winger and a full back. Defend with the same number of forwards but no winger.

If the ball goes very quickly from the attacking scrum half to full back or winger, your role as number 8 is to try to run in directly behind the ball carrier. If the ball carrier angles the attacking run toward the posts, you may find that a switch pass will put you into space. Once you have passed the ball, you must follow it in fast support. On the other hand, if the ball carrier must take contact, all your other options—bumping, driving and rolling—will come into play.

Success Goal = 4 scores out of 5

attempts ____

Success Check

- Ball in quickly behind back-row defence ____
- Ball moves fast through contact area ____
- Wide, stable stance in contact ____
- Bump and roll to show ball to support players ____
- If ball carrier goes into contact, drive in quickly ____
- Left defensive flanker pulled toward ball for fast attack ____
- Accurate pass to overlapping player ____
- Decisive and quick to point of contact ____
- Eyes open, look for attacking opportunities ____

To Increase Difficulty

- Add a left wing defender.
- Add an extra defender 10 metres behind the scrummage.

To Decrease Difficulty

- If you've added an extra defender, have that defender move farther away from the scrum.
- Make the back-row defenders start on hands and knees.

5. Line-Out Deflection: Back Row

You may have a responsibility in the line-out to try to win the ball cleanly for a strike by the backs or a peeling sequence by the forwards. In either case your priority is to win a controlled ball using two hands, knocking it gently down into a target area close by. From there it will be moved away quickly by the scrum half or driven to the corner of the line-out by a peeling forward.

You may also catch the ball and drive forward with support from forwards on either side. This is done to tie in the opposition back row for a follow-up attack either close by or in the middle of the field.

To practise peeling at the line-out, the forward designated to catch the peel must join in the practice. Although traditionally a prop forward from the front of the line-out catches the peel, it is better to use either of the two locks, who are used to catching a ball in close-contact situations. Your props can follow up the play to protect the ball carrier in any contact situation. Make sure to always stand the correct distance from the touch line when you practise your line-out sequences.

In this drill you have to choose one of your three options. If you tap down to the scrum half, you must follow up the ensuing attack. If you tap down for a peel, you may be able to stand out from the next contact situation to receive the ball for a follow-up attack. If you catch and drive, you must keep the ball safe and strong until a teammate drives in to take it from your hands.

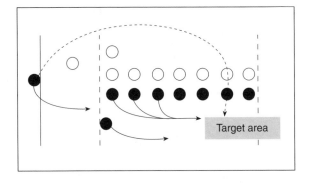

Success Goal = 4 scores out of 5 attempts with accurate execution ___

✔ Success Check

- Ball moves quickly behind defence ___
- Clear signals ___
- Hands ready and above shoulders, inside foot forward, weight on rear foot ___
- Jump high and toward line of touch ___
- When tapping:
  Ball drops about 1 metre out of line-out ___
- When catching:
  Fingers spread, hands close together ___
  Pull ball down quickly to chest ___
  Bend knees, sink hips on wide base to land ___

To Increase Difficulty

- Begin to add defenders to the practice, starting with an opposition.
- Have equal number of defenders and attackers.

To Decrease Difficulty

- Have more attackers than defenders.
- Use tackle shields in the defence.

6. Spiralling the Pass: Scrum Half

You will need a selection of rugby balls and another player to catch your passes. Work together in an area big enough for you to send out a range of passes of different lengths.

Start away from the ball, and walk in to place the rear foot behind the ball. Stride sideways with the front foot and point it in the direction of the pass. Reach down and spread the fingers wide on the passing hand. Use only the index finger and thumb on the guiding hand. Bend at the knees and sink at the hips with weight on the rear foot. Sweep the ball away in one smooth movement, transferring the weight from rear to front (see figure 8.3). Follow the ball through with the hands, finish by pointing at the ball receiver.

Success Goal = 5 accurate passes to left, 5 to right ___

✔ Success Check

- Do not pick up ball ___
- Rear foot behind ball, front foot in direction of pass ___
- Fingers spread wide ___
- Use only index finger and thumb of guiding hand ___
- Bend knees, sink at hips, weight on rear foot ___
- Transfer weight from rear to front ___
- Sweep in one smooth movement ___
- Hands follow through ___

To Increase Difficulty

- Scatter 10 rugby balls in an area. Run to each ball and pass to a receiver.
- Receiver moves about, requiring passes at various lengths and directions.

To Decrease Difficulty

- Talk through the action sequence and then do it.
- Place 10 balls 1 metre apart in a line. Walk up the row and pass to a partner who is following at a set distance.

7. Controlling the Ball: Scrum Half

Work in a grid about 15 metres square to practise passing skills.

a. One player rolls a ball at you and another catches your pass. Control the ball and pass. Remember to keep your fingers spread, the guide hand touching the ball with only the fingertips. Sweep the ball away from the ground without picking it up. Transfer your weight from the rear to front foot as you pass. Point your front foot in the direction of the pass. Follow through with both hands to finish pointing at the receiver.

b. The player who delivers the ball to you follows and tries to knock down the pass. Use this drill to practise passing under extreme pressure from a defender who is trying to tackle you. Begin with no pressure, then defender tries to knock down the pass and finally defender tries to tackle you. A flick or pop pass is a good pass to use in this situation.

Success Goal = 10 smooth passes in total, 5 to left and 5 to right ___

Success Check

- Fingers spread, only fingertips of guide hand touch ___
- Sweep ball without picking it up ___
- Transfer weight from rear to front ___
- Front foot points in direction of pass ___
- Both hands follow through ___
- Pop pass: look for target, flick ball into target ___
- Legs bent ___

To Increase Difficulty

- Partner follows the ball after it has been rolled along the ground.
- Partner selects the direction in which to pass *after* the ball is rolled.
- Partner tries to knock ball down as it is passed.

To Decrease Difficulty

- Partner calls the direction in which to pass *before* the ball is rolled and selects the type of pass.

8. Varying Passes: Scrum Half

Practise with two other players in a space wide enough for you to exchange passes of different lengths. One player acts as a feeder and should call out different signals for the type of pass you should send out to the other player, for example "Point first-long". You then step into the ball and deliver the required pass.

Success Goal = 10 out of 10 smooth passes ___

Success Check

- Fingers at right angles to seam, spread wide ___
- Guide hand fingertips just touching ball ___
- Step in with rear foot, stride toward receiver with front foot ___
- Sweep ball smoothly ___

To Increase Difficulty

- One player selects the direction (left or right) in which to pass after the ball is rolled.
- The feeder follows the rolling ball.
- Feeder tries to knock the ball down as it is passed.

To Decrease Difficulty

- Feeder selects the direction in which to pass before the ball is rolled.
- Feeder walks after the rolling ball and makes no effort to knock the ball down.

9. Passing Options: Scrum Half

To practise your passing options, pass to a group of players who decide the type of pass they wish to receive. The players line up behind you in two lines, line 1 and line 2. At no time are you allowed to look behind you. A number of balls are placed on the ground in front of you.

So that you and the receivers react quickly, your coach indicates who will run to receive the pass by calling out two numbers: the first number is the line and the second the player in that line; for example "2, 1" indicates that the first player from line number two should run to receive the pass. The other player always follows in support.

The nearest runner will tell you the side (left or right) and the distance (close, middle or far); for example, the runner may give the signal "right, far" to indicate that the runner will appear to your right and will require a long, spiralling pass. Deliver the ball accurately to the receiver.

Success Goal = 10 out of 10 crisp, accurate passes of correct type ____

Success Check
- Wait for coach's signal ____
- Do not reach for ball until you know passing direction ____
- Spiral passes: sweep ball smoothly ____
- Flick passes: move ball through hands quickly ____

To Increase Difficulty
- Runners call the direction and type of pass a little later.
- Coach delivers the ball to you as the signal is called.

To Decrease Difficulty
- Coach and runners give signals very early.

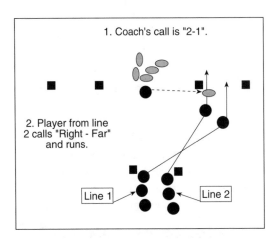

1. Coach's call is "2-1".

2. Player from line 2 calls "Right - Far" and runs.

Line 1   Line 2

10. Kicking Over the Forwards: Scrum Half

Mark out a 5-metre square, about 25 metres away from the kicking area. Try to kick the ball high and land it in the square. Remember the correct kicking sequence: "Plant, scoop, step, kick".

10. Kicking Over the Forwards: Scrum Half

Mark out a 5-metre square, about 25 metres away from the kicking area. Try to kick the ball high and land it in the square. Remember the correct kicking sequence: "Plant, scoop, step, kick".

Success Goal = 7 out of 10 successful kicks ___

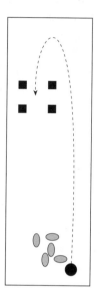

Success Check
- Smooth step-kick sequence ___
- Wide, low stance with right foot planted firmly ___
- Bend knees, sink at hips, scoop ___
- Right hand along and underneath seam ___
- Stride across with non-kicking foot ___
- Drop ball, seam along bootlaces ___
- Kick with right leg through long axis of ball ___

To Increase Difficulty
- Place 6 balls in 2 groups of 3, groups 5 metres apart. Walk to one group; plant, scoop, step, kick; then turn and repeat at the other group.
- Alternate kicking with left and right foot.

To Decrease Difficulty
- Use 6 balls in a line 1 metre apart. Walk to each ball and kick.
- Make the target bigger.

11. Kicking for Position: Scrum Half

Set out a target square along a touch line. Do not set them too far to begin with. Master accuracy first, then you can begin to try much longer kicks.

Success Goal = 7 out of 10 kicks through the square ___

Success Check
- Wide, low stance; right foot planted firmly ___
- Bend knees, sink at hips, scoop up ball ___
- Right hand along and underneath seam ___
- Stride across with non-kicking foot ___
- Drop ball, seam along bootlaces ___
- Kick with right leg through long axis of ball ___

To Increase Difficulty
- Coach calls "left" or "right" to indicate the target touch line.

To Decrease Difficulty
- Practise 5 kicks to the right, then 5 to the left in your own time trying to kick the ball anywhere across the touch line.

12. Running From the Scrum Half Position

The role of the scrum half at the scrum is to threaten the defence, especially the back row. To do this you must have speed and vision. Practise in a narrow (about 10-metre) channel against a defender who is kneeling in the flanker's position and an attacking number 8 who will follow your attacking run. As soon as you pick up the ball and run, so too can the defender.

Success Goal = 7 out of 10 attacks that score ___

Success Check
• Pick up ball quickly ___
• Stay low, be prepared to be tackled ___
• Run at top speed, eyes open ___
• Look for opportunities to pass to your number 8 ___

To Increase Difficulty
• Add a full back to begin to make a defensive screen.

To Decrease Difficulty
• Bring your own back row into the practice.

13. Pass Length: Fly Half

In this simple practice you receive the ball from the scrum half and have two support runners. One of them will run as a centre, and the other will run from depth and appear in the gap between you and your centre partner. You must make an instantaneous decision to catch and pop pass to the "intruder" in the line or to catch and pass slightly farther across to your centre partner.

You can now develop to working along two channels side by side. Use the first ball to one side and then slow down after the first pass to allow your support players to regroup behind you to the other side. Receive the second ball from the scrum half and pass in the other direction.

Sometimes other players in the team, without the ball, will demand you pass to them in different ways. You can simulate this by having your coach make the passing decision for you as ball carrier.

In this practice you attack close to the forwards, your coach decides which of your two support runners will receive the ball and also the type of pass. No matter which pass you are to make, you must move the defender who is coming at you away from the direction of your intended pass. If you pass too early or drift away, the defender will run by you and tackle the next player with the ball.

Success Goal = 10 successful passes to each support player ___

Success Check
• Alter defender's running line before pass ___
• Pop pass: very little arm movement, flick with wrists and fingers ___
• Longer pass: push ball across at chest height, much longer arm movements ___
• Run toward space behind defender ___
• Accurate pass of correct power and length ___

To Increase Difficulty
• Coach calls the type of pass as you receive the ball.
• Coach decides which support player should receive the pass.
• Allow the defender to start closer to the fly half.

To Decrease Difficulty
• Defender starts farther away and directly ahead of you.
• Coach calls the type of pass before the scrum half delivers the ball to you.

14. Beating the Defence: Fly Half

The first defender running at you is only the first problem in a rather complicated equation. Rugby union always presents an attack with a multi-layered defence.

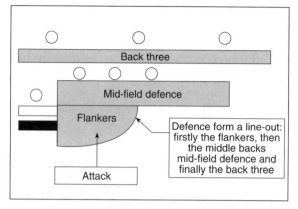

Defence form a line-out: firstly the flankers, then the middle backs mid-field defence and finally the back three

If you go beyond the defence set up by the forwards, you then have to beat your opposite number who is part of the mid-field defence. If you break this line of defence, then you have the back three to contend with. Putting a player into space is only the first step. As a fly half, you must understand where you will go next and what will happen should your plays be successful. If you pass the ball early, you are an ideal player to loop around behind the ball carrier and support, in case you are required again in the attack. You then become one of the support players running from depth, and you may have other players in your team running alongside you.

Breaking down layers in the defence is difficult. Begin simply, play 3 vs. 2 and develop this to 4 vs. 3. When you get to this stage begin to shape the defence to resemble different layers, for example line the 3 defenders up as a triangle—2 at the front and 1 behind. Can you penetrate or go round the first pair of defenders and then beat the last defender to score?

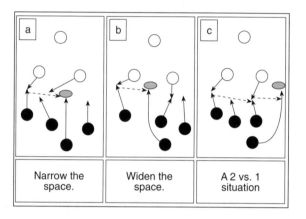

a — Narrow the space.

b — Widen the space.

c — A 2 vs. 1 situation

Your options are simple:

* Narrow the space between the defenders, and put a runner around the outside edge (see figure a).

* Widen the space between the defenders, and put a runner coming from depth into that gap (see figure b).

* Work hard for a 2 vs. 1 situation, and put one of the other players around the edge (see figure c).

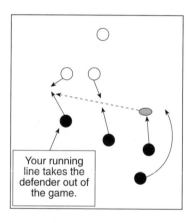

Your running line takes the defender out of the game.

As first-pass receiver, you must prevent the first defender from drifting across the field. Your running line and your subsequent actions should prevent the defender from being effective in the defence. It is then up to the other runners to go past the next defender and attack the last player in the channel.

You must practise to both left and right, and you must work hard to get back in the game as soon as you have released the ball. You may be required farther upfield in a scoring position.

Success Goal = 5 scores from 5 fast-moving attacks ___

✔ Success Check

- Pull defences out of shape ___
- Draw first defender toward you, or use dummy pass and attack last defender ___
- Pass quickly if running line moves defender away from pass ___
- Communicate with support runners ___

◢ To Increase Difficulty

- When your coach decides that you are ready, play full tackles.
- Bring the rear defender a little closer to the front line of defence.

To Decrease Difficulty ◥

- Assign a support runner to each defender. You have to find the free player—communication helps.

15. Kicking for Possession: Fly Half

Mark out a number of squares to simulate kicking down a certain line (e.g., the 15-metre line) or kicking diagonally toward the posts. Have your scrum half feed the ball to you so you can practise collecting the ball, stepping forward and kicking. Try to kick so that the ball remains in the air for a specific number of seconds. Go for height and accuracy first, and then progress to distance. Alternate among the squares until you can land the ball in them regularly. Gradually work farther away from the squares as your accuracy improves and gradually add a number of defenders to put pressure on your kick.

When you intend to kick the ball, signal to your scrum half as early as possible for the ball to be passed to you while you are in a stationary position. Your scrum half should pass the ball to just in front of you so that you can walk forward, gather the ball, retain your balance and kick accurately.

Success Goal = 7 out of 10 successful kicks into each square that stay in air for specified time ___

✔ Success Check

- Walk forward, gather pass and kick ___
- High, accurate kicks ___
- Signal to scrum half early ___
- Do not kick while running ___
- Sidestep then kick if the defender is very close to you ___

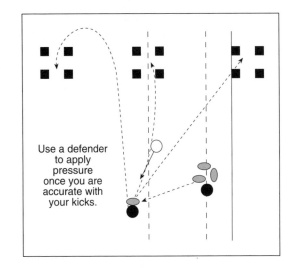

Use a defender to apply pressure once you are accurate with your kicks.

To Increase Difficulty

- Scrum half follows the pass to pressure the kicker by running across the line of vision.
- As you receive the kick, the coach decides which square to aim for.
- Add an extra defender to chase the fly half. Defenders should be at the same distances at which they would be if they were running from ruck, maul, line-out or scrum.
- Add two attacking centres to chase after the kick; defence adds a player to act as full back.
- If the centres arrive at the same time as the ball, the game plays on and each side tries to score over the opposition goal line.

To Decrease Difficulty

- Coach designates the square *before* the scrum half passes the ball.
- Scrum half walks quickly after the pass to touch you before you kick.
- Make the target areas much bigger.

MIDDLE FIVE SUCCESS SUMMARY

The middle five players in the team act as the link between those who provide the ball—the front five—and those who are put into positions to strike for the score—the back five. The back row and half backs who make up the middle five are the ball users, pinning down the defence and creating space for others. They also play a major role on team defence. Because the middle five must possess good all-around skills, it's important to practice body and ball movement skills. Have another player or a coach evaluate your skills using the Keys to Success fundamentals used in figures 8.1 through 8.4.

STEP 9

THE BACK FIVE: THE FINISHERS

The back five is comprised of the centres, wingers and full back. These players react to the attacking situations set up for them by the rest of the team. It is they who follow up an initial attempt by others, to break down the defence and often become the players who score the tries.

Centres

The main role of the two centres is to create space for players overlapping on the outside. To do this, they must understand effective running lines and possess good handling and contact skills. Centres should be able to ride tackles and still be able to make controlled passes. In addition, the most dangerous centres are fast and have good evasive skills. Many of the skills detailed in Steps 2 and 3 are essentials for the centre.

Centres often carry the ball very close to the opposition, where the skills to cope with the defensive pressure are essential. Centres sometimes have to make contact with an opponent; they should be fully prepared for contact situations. Good centres can ride contact situations or can burst through them and play the ball in behind the defence or buy time for the support to arrive. Step 6 discussed contact skills in more detail.

If you have good peripheral vision and are skilful, you may make a good centre. The ability to take in visual information over a wide angle allows you to watch the ball as it works its way toward you and, at the same time, the defenders arriving to try to stop you.

Although many players have good peripheral vision naturally, there are practices that may help you notice more detail of the actions of players working in your field of vision (see Drill 1). To check your present field of vision, stand 5 metres from two corner flags that are 5 metres apart. Gradually move these flags apart until each flag is at the edge of your vision. Measure the distance between to determine your current field of vision. Regular measurement will tell you if your training methods are also helping to extend your field of vision.

How to Create Space

When creating space, you should look at the defence before you receive the ball and take up your usual alignment every time your team win possession. Make your decisions early and stick to them. Depending on the defence, catch the ball early or move wide and catch it late in its flight. If the gap is in front of you, move into it and then move the ball away from any covering defence. If the gap is in front of another player, deliver the ball to take best advantage of the space. Remember to support any pass to take best advantage of any opportunity.

Although one of your main priorities is to make space around the edge of the defence, for your winger, you should also be able to create gaps between the centres in the opposition defence to allow a player arriving from depth to penetrate the opposition back line or for you to work the ball in behind their defence.

Every time you line up at scrum or line-out, you and the other backs form a series of triangles. These shapes must be copied in practice, so that you become used to the different angles at which these players would enter your attacking line (see diagram 9.1). Always start your support runners in the positions they would occupy during a match these vary according to the attacking situation.

The non-ball carrying centre can also help the ball carrier to widen or close the gap in front of you. Remember, the defence reacts to both your running lines. If you wish to widen the gap, run so that the distance between you and your partner becomes wider as you near the defence. To narrow the gap,

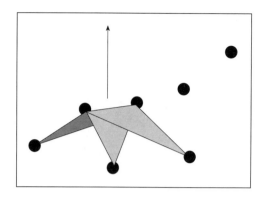

Diagram 9.1 A series of attacking triangles.

run closer together as you near the defence. At the same time, other players who are going to enter the attack line should know what you are trying to achieve and should run to arrive between you and your partner if you are widening the gap, or to the outside of your partner if you are narrowing it and wish to play an overlap move.

If your support players run as too flat a line, you will have only one passing option. Support players should run 2 or 3 metres back from *you* before you pass the ball, so that you can see all possible receivers and accurately deliver the ball to the player who is running in a gap.

How to Ride the Tackle

When your team wins the ball you will have the opportunity to attempt to score . You won't always have a clean run through a gap, and mostly, you will be faced with a tackler. If there is no one in a better position to receive a pass, you will have to take on the defender and may need to resist the tackle.

To successfully ride the tackle, you need to make early decisions. You need to know where you are trying to go to and what will happen next. Try to work out the impact angles so that you can use your opponent's force to move you away from the tackle.

Hold the ball safely in both hands close to your chest, and keep low as you run and look for the spaces ahead of you. Accelerate hard and try to avoid any tacklers. As the tackle comes in, lean over the top of the tackler, lower your body and move away by bumping into and bouncing off from the tackler's shoulder. Keep the momentum of the attack going by either picking up your pace quickly or passing to a support player who is running at speed. (See Step 6 for more on contact skills.)

Wingers

The main requirement for the winger is speed. If you can add agility and strength to your speed, then you have the makings of a good player. You can increase your speed by using the running drills in Step 3. You also have to learn to run at pace with control while moving your body quickly off a straight running line.

If your centres have done their job well, you should be running at pace each time you receive the ball. Pick up speed quickly and attack the space. At the same time, watch what any defenders are doing and constantly look for support. If you know that you are likely to be tackled, slow down to allow your support to catch up or run at an angle slightly away from the touch line so that your support is nearer to you.

Unless you have only a short distance to go to the goal line, you first should head toward the covering full back and then accelerate hard, off toward the corner. This should check the defenders' run so that you can more easily win the race for the goal line.

It is very unusual for wingers to have to beat only one player. Wingers normally first have to accelerate past their immediate opponent and then beat the last line of defence. You should always try to practise under such pressure. You may also need to acquire skills for beating tacklers, especially close to the corner flag.

As you run with the ball over even a short distance, the defence in front of you can quickly change. You may sometimes appear in the back line, away from your normal position, to try to penetrate the defensive line. Here too the defence in front of you will change and present many different problems. Your role is to be a constant threat to the defence.

Full Back

A full back needs many qualities and skills. You have to be brave, because most of the tackles you make will probably be at full speed and full stretch. You also have to catch, run at speed, kick and play like a centre when you enter the line. Safety in defence is a priority, particularly under a ball that has been kicked high. You should learn to catch with both feet on the ground and while jumping, and to field the ball while you are in the air. You should also learn a variety of kicks (see Step 5). These skills need to be performed under extreme pressure with tacklers approaching from a number of different angles.

When entering the attacking line as a penetrator, you need to time your run to make best use of the attacking opportunity. The classic place for you to join the attack is outside the outside centre. This position pulls the opposing winger toward you, so that you can pass to your own winger to either attempt to score or run the ball downfield.

There is nothing to stop you from running outside the winger if you have the speed. You should consider entering the attacking three-quarter line between the centres, between centre and wing or on the very outside. Situations naturally occur in the game which lead you to attack the spaces in the opposing back line. You may also act as decoy runner or as an extra fly half to take the ball up the narrow side with your winger and centre in support.

One of your main priorities is to make quick decisions. Will you pass? run? kick? Your team's strategy and tactics will make some of these decisions for you, but you should be prepared to make full use of any ball you get from the opposition from a kick or in contact.

Of all the positions in the team, yours has the most potential for attacking the opposition especially when they have lost the ball from either a handling error or by an aimless or mis-directed kick. This type of attack is called a counter-attack. Your option is to run and pass, run and dummy pass or kick. Your first priority is to make a decision. Then pull any defenders away from the attack area. If appropriate, pass to someone else in a better position, or run at the forwards to check their advance and then pass to the space you will have created. There will also be opportunities for you to use your dummy pass to send chasers the wrong way and also to kick either for touch if you are under pressure, or downfield to chase.

Table 9.1

Centre

Individual—Good all-round vision. Very strong in shoulders and lower body to withstand high-speed impacts. Good pace and power. Well-developed handling skills. Good understanding of the game.

At the set piece—Understands when to close and when to maintain the distance to opponents. Misshapes the defence and creates gaps. Knows the most effective defensive systems and how to apply them.

Loose—Takes advantage of all opportunities provided by other players. Creates opportunities for the finishers. Understands how to create space and stop defences. Running and evasive skills constantly threaten the defence. Strong, safe tackles in defence prevent the ball carrier from crossing the tackle line.

Winger

Individual—Speed above all, plus power, aggression and understanding. Strong in the shoulders and lower body to withstand high-speed impacts.

At the set piece—Looks for the ball (especially left winger) to hit gaps in the defence or to help centres create overlap attacks. Catches attacking kicks. Kicks accurately upfield for distance or touch.

Loose—Scores when given any opportunity.

Full back

Individual—Strong in shoulders and lower body. Good pace and power.

At the set piece—Marks and tackles any player who threatens to penetrate or overlap the defence. Safe and strong when defending against ball carriers and kicks.

Loose—Threatens the defence by joining attack out wide or through the middle. Looks for attacking opportunities. Organises the defence from behind. Marks and tackles opponents who break through the tackle area. Strong, safe tackles. Accurate, safe fielding of kicks and returns to touch or downfield.

BACK FIVE SUCCESS STOPPERS

The following are common errors made by the Cente, Winger and Full Back. Have a trained instructor watch you for these problems.

Error	Correction
Centre	
1. You do not release the pass under pressure for fear of it being knocked down by the defender.	1. Stay back from the passer a little more as you are running (be able to read the number on the player's shirt), either by delaying your run or standing a little deeper at the start. This will give you time to catch and pass the ball.
2. The player collecting your pass in the gap always seems to drop it.	2. Take the power out of the pass—lob the ball into the space at the side of you. This will put the ball at eye level for the receiver, who can then accelerate onto the ball.
3. Riding contact seems impossible; each time you try it you are brought down.	3. When you go into contact, make sure that you keep your legs away from the tackler by leaning over your front foot. Don't make contact unless you have no other alternatives: Try a running line that will move the defender away from the intended tackle area and then swerve or sidestep past the would-be tackler.
4. Making passes is difficult in heavily defended areas.	4. Always carry the ball in two hands so that you can take any opportunity to pass. Remember, your priority is to create space for other people to exploit and so your running lines should misshape the defence, as soon as this happens let the ball go to another player.
5. You are slow to decide what to do next, and therefore your attacking opportunities are constantly being shut down.	5. Learn your own strengths and your team's strengths, and play to them. Understand your options, and stick to your decisions.
Winger	
1. You are given space on the outside but always want to step back inside to beat the defence.	1. Are you playing on the correct side of the team? Normally, left-handed or -footed people should play on the left, and right-handed or -footed people on the right. If you are on the correct side, you should work on your running speed using sprinting drills and practise running on the outside with some of the drills in this chapter.

Error	Correction
Winger (continued)	
2. You do not seem to be able to score the classic winger's try (a try scored at the corner with defenders left lying on the ground after vain attempts to stop the score).	2. Practise beating a defender on the outside near the corner flag and then diving in to score. Once successful, put two tackle bags half a metre apart at the corner, and dive in between the bags to score.
3. You can score within 22 metres of the goal line with ease, but never seem to score from farther out.	3. You need to work on your speed over a greater distance. Normally you should sprint no farther than 40 metres, but occasional practice over a greater distance will not harm. Work on acceleration over short distances and then on holding the speed for as long as you can.
4. The one-on-one situation presents many problems for you, and you score less than half of the tries you should when faced with one defender.	4. Develop your sidestepping and swerving skills. Work against a live defence and constantly alter your running line of approach until you find the one that pulls the defender out of position enough for you to score.
Full Back	
1. You do not seem to be able to consistently catch the high ball.	1. Keep your eyes on the ball and turn sideways to the chasers. Point your fingers upward, palms facing you and elbows together. Reach as the ball comes down and pull it to your chest as you sink down from the knees.
2. Counter-attacks are ineffective because the defence is always there to stop them.	2. Learn the basic counter-attack patterns. The underlying principle is that the ball has to move out into space as quickly as possible, but any covering players—including the pack of forwards—must be first taken away from the intended attack area.
3. You always arrive late when called into the three-quarter line to create an overlap.	3. Make sure that your initial position for entering the line is not too far away for your pace. You may start in this position, but as soon as the defence begin to watch the ball, move quickly a lot closer to where you intend to join the line.
4. You always seem to be under pressure while you are waiting to catch the high ball.	4. Learn to jump and catch it. Once you are in the air, no one can tackle you.
5. Your defence is constantly caught out when your opponents bring the full back into the three-quarter line as an extra attacker.	5. Choose one of the following systems of defence and stick to it. • Drift across so that the defender takes the next player out from usual. • Full back takes full back. • Winger steps in for the full back, defending full back takes winger.

DRILLS

1. Developing All-Round Vision: Centre

While you look at a partner, another player stands about 10 metres away to the side, just inside the widest angle of your sight. Continuously pass to and receive a pass from your partner, while the third player gives you visual signals (raising left, right or both arms), which you must try to identify. Practise to both sides, and constantly check to see if your field of vision is becoming wider.

Success Goal = Correctly identify signal 10 times out of 10 ____

Success Check
• Concentrate on ball ____
• Head still, but use your eyes ____

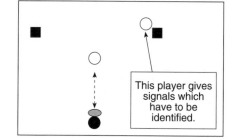

This player gives signals which have to be identified.

To Increase Difficulty
• Move forward as you handle the ball, first walking then jogging. The signaller moves as well.
• Signals are given just before you catch and just after you pass the ball.

To Decrease Difficulty
• Only one signal should be given.
• Move the signaller well into your line of vision.

2. Passing Under Pressure: Centre

You will pressure the defence only if you put yourself under pressure as well. To practise the pressure pass, a defender tries to knock the ball out of your hands. Set up a narrow channel approximately 10 metres wide and 15 metres long with two defenders at the far end. The first ball carrier must carry the ball close to the first defender before the pass is made.

Begin by practising without the defender. Try to catch and pass within one to two paces. As soon as you can do this, put the defenders in place. You should always feel pressure from the defender as you pass, so you must be close to your opponent before you pass.

Success Goal = 10 out of 10 quick, accurate passes, each within two strides ____

Success Check
- Work fast until you reach match speed ____
- Reach to catch and push ball across chest ____
- Work close to defender ____
- Do not rush pass ____
- Reduce speed as ball approaches to keep some space between you and defender ____

To Increase Difficulty
- Defender moves to open side, into the passer's blind spot.
- Defender tries to tackle the ball carrier (when your coach tells you that you are ready).
- Work down the channel, making passes first from the left and then from the right. Use a number of defenders.

To Decrease Difficulty
- Run a little slower so that you create a little more space and time between yourself and the defender.

3. Feeding a Player Running From Depth: Centre

This drill will allow you to practice skills which widen or narrow the gaps in the defence so that other players in your team, such as the wingers or full back, can take advantage of that attacking opportunity. You should work with the fly half and your co-centre plus one of the other players mentioned previously. Practice in a channel which is 15 metres wide and about 20 metres long. Always involve two defenders who are the focus of the attack. They would stand as if they were opposing the attacking centres. When the attackers launch the attack a number of triangles are formed with the centres and one of the wingers or full back. It is the rear point of the triangle who will normally penetrate the defence. The front two points (centres) have to widen or narrow the gap ahead to allow this to happen. One of the centres must carry the ball at the defender to fix the defence. Once this happens the other attacking centre can then run to affect the shape of the defence. The rear player then runs at any gap and receives a pass from the ball carrier.

Success Goal = 10 out of 10 successful passing sequences ____

Success Check
- Constant, reliable, accurate communication ____
- Run quickly, but with control ____
- Support runners arrive running at gaps ____
- Soft passes popped into space ____
- Support runners both present target ____

To Increase Difficulty
- Allow defenders to defend as they wish.
- Roll the ball into the channel for the first centre to pick up and then attack.

To Decrease Difficulty
- Two defenders follow and only shadow the centres.

4. Riding the Contact: Centre

Make sure you have mastered the contact drills in Step 6. You should avoid contact as much as possible, but if you know that a tackler is about to collide with you, you may be able to use that force to your advantage. This drill gives you practise riding contact. Play in a channel no wider than 8 metres so that it is difficult to avoid contact. The channel can be as long as you wish, depending on the number of tacklers available. Tacklers are spaced at 5-metre intervals and hold tackle shields.

Pay attention to the tackler coming at you to anticipate the angle of the hit, and prepare to alter your own body angle or running line to bounce away from the edge of the tackle.

When you start your run, try to check the defender and then go around the tackle. You may sometimes be able to bump and spin, or soak up the force of the hit. Try every trick you know to lessen the defender's power. You must keep moving the ball forward as fast as you can, however.

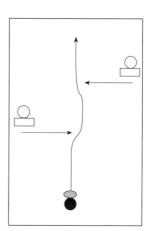

Success Goal = 5 lengths of the channel with little or no stoppage ____

✔ Success Check
• Check defender by running at inside gap ____
• As defender commits to tackle, move feet away and lean inward with shoulder ____
• Bump defender firmly, bounce away, keep running ____

To Increase Difficulty
• Have two defenders approach at once, one from the left and one from the right, to simulate a multi-layered defence.

To Decrease Difficulty
• Widen the channel to give the attacker a little more space on the outside.

5. Beating the Last Line of Defence: Winger

Defenders, especially those in the last line of defence, will be running to tackle you from different angles and directions. You will need a number of defenders to help you with this practice. Begin with touch tackles and gradually develop to full tackling once you have been regularly successful at beating the defence. Play from the 10-metre line toward the goal line, between the 15-metre and touch line.

Each defender is numbered 1, 2 or 3. These defenders each stand by one of the markers as shown in the diagram on page 131. The coach rolls the ball out in front of you into the channel, then calls a number (1, 2 or 3). The indicated player runs into the channel and tries to stop you from scoring on the goal line. Each time the defenders go back to their markers, they change their numbers so that you never know which player will come at you.

Rolling the ball along the ground prevents you from looking at the defenders. As soon as you pick up the ball, you have to make an instantaneous decision about how you will attack the goal line. In this practice, you will be able to use all of the running skills acquired in Step 3.

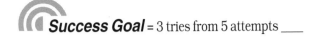 **Success Goal** = 3 tries from 5 attempts ___

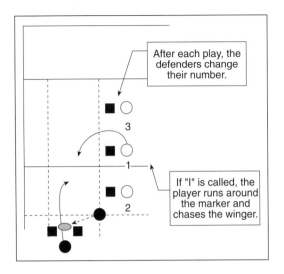

After each play, the defenders change their number.

If "I" is called, the player runs around the marker and chases the winger.

Success Check

- Create space with pace or running line ___
- Dominate defender, do not let defender dominate you ___
- Use running line that keeps defender near 15-metre line before using the open space ___

To Increase Difficulty

- Decrease the distance between the defenders and the attacker.
- Coach rolls the ball farther forward into the channel.

To Decrease Difficulty

- Widen the channel.
- Coach calls the tackler's number before rolling in the ball.

6. Winning the Race for the Corner: Winger

You must have confidence in your ability to beat a defender on the outside. This drill lets you practise with a defender who is always trying to push you out toward the touch line. If you add a change of direction, you can practise the running lines used by most wingers. Use a channel from the half-way line to goal line and between the 15-metre and touch line.

The defender has the ball and passes it to you as a signal to start the race. Once you receive the ball, swerve around the markers as shown in the diagram on page 132. and head for the corner. The defender's marker is placed so that the defensive pressure comes from slightly behind you as you run at the corner flag, to prevent you from dodging infield and to force you to accelerate hard to score in the corner.

Look at the defender only as the ball is delivered to you; looking over your shoulder slows you down. Run through the first two markers quickly but in control, then accelerate hard toward the corner. Unless the defender is standing directly in front of you, concentrate only on winning the race to the goal line.

 **Success Goal** = 10 scores out of 10 attempts ___

Success Check

- Look at defender as ball is delivered ___
- Run quickly but in control, then accelerate hard to score ___
- Concentrate on winning race to goal line ___

To Increase Difficulty

• Stand a tackle bag about 1 metre from the corner flag and on the goal line so that when you
score, you can bump into the tackle bag just
before you put the ball down.

To Decrease Difficulty

• Put the defender's marker a little farther out to
give the ball carrier an advantage.

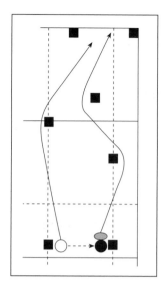

7. Reacting Quickly to the Defence: Winger

Mark out a 5-metre square, 5 metres inside a rectangle that is 15 metres wide and 22 metres
long. Use 4 defenders, the front 2 carrying tackle shields close to the internal square. The other
two players defend the goal line. At the start of this practice, turn your back to the square. The
coach rolls the ball towards you and nominates one of the shield holders to enter the square. You
have to turn round, pick up the ball, beat the first defender in the internal square and then
attack the goal line. The coach calls one of the last two defenders into the rectangle for you to try
to beat for the score.

Check the defender by attacking the space near the touch line, then head quickly for the
space you have created. Sometimes the defender may wrongly anticipate what you are going to
do and create a space; use it to your advantage.

Success Goal = 10 scores out of 10 ___

Success Check
• Run quickly, but with control ___
• Make contact with the first defender on your
terms ___
• Dominate second defender with speed and
running line ___
• Use defender's decisions to your advantage ___

To Increase Difficulty

• Move the line of secondary defenders closer to
the shield holders.

To Decrease Difficulty

• Widen the channel.

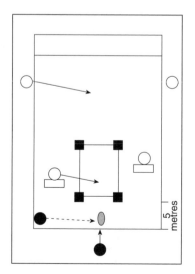

8. Making Quick Decisions: Full Back

In this drill work close to a touch line. A player outside the touch line feeds you the ball by throwing it high or rolling it along the ground. A defender then puts pressure on you as you collect the ball.

Judge the height of the ball and the closeness of the defender; if necessary, jump to catch the ball. If there is little space between you and the defender, you may wish to kick the ball to touch. If farther away from the defender, you may choose to keep the ball on the field and kick for position. If there is little pressure, you may decide to run and counter-attack with the feeder of the ball in support. If you decide to run, try to widen the space near the touch line. Your support runner will then have space to receive a pass. Although in a practice you can try different ways of beating the defender in the game you would run only if you had sufficient support to sustain the attack.

Once you begin to make good decisions, add an extra defender and two more attackers to help you, one attacker running back from a centre position and the other from the wing. The nearest defender can put more pressure on you: If you are caught as you land from jumping and catching the ball, your two support players can practise going in and stripping the ball from your arms. If the ball is thrown too deep for the defender to exert severe pressure, practise setting up a counter-attack move.

Success Goal = 8 out of 10 actions successfully completed ____

Success Check
• Judge height of ball and closeness of defender ____
• If kicking for touch, do so quickly ____
• If kicking for position, high and accurate kick ____
• If running with ball, try to widen space near touch line ____

To Increase Difficulty
• Move the defender closer.
• Move the full back farther from the touch line.

To Decrease Difficulty
• Coach throws the ball to the full back's rather than the chaser's advantage.

9. Joining the Attack: Full Back

This practice helps you time your run into the line so that you can be most effective when attacking. Your first problem is to look at the three defenders and decide which of the gaps between them you will attack. Call a signal early and indicate the gap you will run at. The ball carrier then makes sure that you receive the ball as you hit that gap. The ball carrier must attack the tackle line (where the two sets of back lines would collide in a game); you must support that player with the intention of receiving a pass that will put you across the tackle line. Give a second signal to the ball carrier as you approach the line to indicate the type of pass you want.

Once you have mastered the timing, add a defender behind the current defence. Time your run to take the pass as the attackers close in on the tackle line. If everything is timed correctly, you should run through the gap and be able to draw the back player toward you so that you can pass to the outside player to score.

 **Success Goal** = 8 scores out of 10
attacks ____

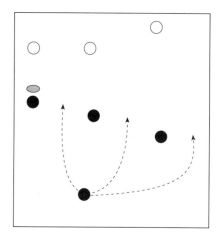

✔ **Success Check**
• Run with purpose and determination ____
• Target defenders' inside shoulders ____
• Support attacking player ____
• Signal the type of pass you want ____

To Increase Difficulty
• Defenders may switch the players they're defending, as they would in a game, so that sometimes a defender is directly in front of the attacking full back. The ball carrier must then put the ball into the hands of a player running at a space.

To Decrease Difficulty
• Defenders only shadow the front three attackers, leaving the full back always free to cross the tackle line.

10. Counter-Attack: Full Back and Wingers

Counter-attack requires a mental attitude that must be practised. Classic counter-attacks stem from possession gained from a badly aimed kick by the opposition, but you can counter-attack from any situation. To practise basic counter-attacking patterns, your coach should throw the ball to your team in two different ways.

The first throw for you to practise is straight upfield along the 15-metre line. The full back runs toward the nearest touch line and switch passes with the winger, who then joins with the other winger to attack down the opposite side of the field. The full back's running line leading up to the switch should take any defenders away from this attack area.

The second throw goes into mid-field. If the full back catches the ball while running at pace, the defenders from the opposite side of the field will probably be unable to reach the attack area, so the full back should head straight for the attack area with the open-side winger as support.

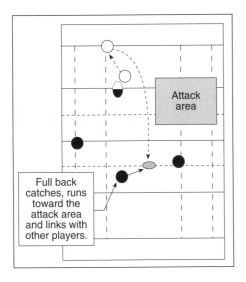

Full back catches, runs toward the attack area and links with other players.

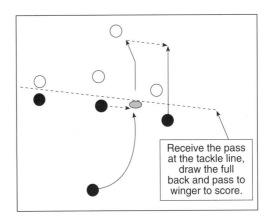

Receive the pass at the tackle line, draw the full back and pass to winger to score.

Success Goal = 4 scores from 8 out of 10 counter-attacks that enter the attack area ____

Success Check

• Keep eyes on ball ____
• Make decision after catching ____
• To switch pass, drag defender away from attack area ____

To Increase Difficulty

• Add another defender to chase the ball in the air.
• Move the defenders closer to the attacking full back.
• Start with 3 vs. 2 and gradually add attackers and defenders until you are practising with the middle and back five.

To Decrease Difficulty

• Allow the first defender to chase only the attacking full back, no other attacker.
• Instead of having only a 1-player advantage, give the attacking side three more players than the defence.

BACK FIVE SUCCESS SUMMARY

The role of the back-five players is to take advantage of the space made for them by the other 10 players in the team. They must have good handling ability and speed allied with an awareness of space and an understanding of how to make the best use of it. It is they who also may have to unlock the defence by attacking an area or an individual, thus creating other attacking opportunities should they not score.

Each player should understand the concepts of creating space and be able to perform this skill when under pressure. Their roles are to turn all opportunities into devastating and irresistible attacks especially when the opposition turn over the ball in contact or by aimless kicking.

Safety in defence is also of paramount importance and the players must understand their role in all of the different ways of defending and have a desire to prevent the opposition from scoring by making aggressive tackles which stop the attack and give their team the opportunity to turn over the ball.

MINI-UNITS: ATTACKING IN SMALL GROUPS

Players in a number of positions constantly interact with each other during a game. These players often make up trios, for example, the forwards in the front row and those in the back row. There are trios of backs: the fly half and two centres in mid-field, and the full back and two wingers behind them. If you are a member of one of these mini-units, you should practise together to become "a team within the team". If your mini-unit is efficient, you will add strength to the other sections of the team.

Sometimes the mini-unit works together to create space for other players. In turn, those players also may work together to release other players into the attack. An example of a move that requires coordination between two mini-units is a back-row move that releases the mid-field three players, who work hard to create space for the back three. The mid-field and back three mini-units will line up in an M shape to make most effective use of any space or gap.

If you have the ball in attack, other players become involved, so that a number of other mini-units form as a match develops. As a ball carrier in open play or as the scrum half from the base of a ruck or maul, you will normally have two or three support players to set up the next attack. These mini-units are not prearranged; they occur quite spontaneously during the game.

When the ball comes slowly from the ruck or maul or the ball carrier faces a covering defence, the attack sometimes struggles to be effective. At times like this you need to apply the basic principles of playing in small units discussed in the following section. These principles rely heavily on the discipline of the support and the vision of the ball carrier.

Developing Mini-Unit Skills Using Channels

Practising all your positional skills and individual skills together as a trio will help your mini-unit un-

derstand how to work together, so that when you play the game under pressure you will react instinctively to each other. You should therefore aim to run as a group during skill practice sessions so that you can specifically practise attacking ploys centred around your positions.

In the early stages of learning, you should practise in channels 5 metres wide and 22 metres long, without any defenders (see diagram 10.1). Once all members of your mini-unit react correctly to the ball carrier, add defenders. To begin with, respond to instructions from your coach so that the ball carrier or support runners can practise finding the gap in the defence. When you can do this successfully, allow the defenders to try to stop the attack in any way they can.

If you are the ball carrier at the outside, run forward and inward toward the next channel, but do not enter it. The players in the other channels must keep their running lines parallel to the touch lines (see diagram 10.2).

When you reach the edge of the channel, you have a number of options:

1. Pop pass into the first channel to the first receiver.

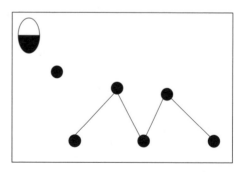

Diagram 10.1 Form a letter "M" shape.

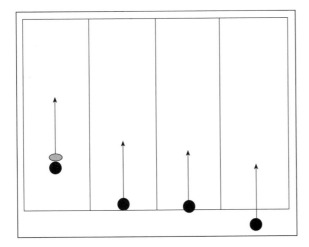

Diagram 10.2 Unopposed to begin with.

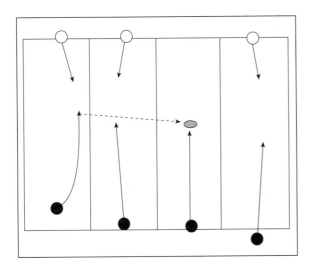

Diagram 10.3 Support runners are parallel to touch line.

2. Miss pass (skip over) across the next channel to the second receiver (see diagram 10.3).
3. Miss pass across two channels to the third receiver.

The player who catches the pass has another set of options available, including a pass back, a miss pass further out or penetration through a hole in the defence. The underlying principle of all of these attacks is that the non-ball carriers must run at spaces between the defenders ahead of them. The channels at this stage represent spaces.

You can now begin to change positions in the channels in order to practise decoy running and switching the direction of the attack. If you run

from your original channel into another channel with the ball, the player occupying that channel takes up the space you left. This ensures that your attack remains running parallel to the touch lines. At the point of the cross-over, you have a number of options:

1. Switch pass (see diagram 10.4).
2. Receive a pass back as a looping player.
3. Pop pass to the outside channel (see diagram 10.5).
4. Miss pass to the second receiver on the outside
5. Dummy any of those passes and run through

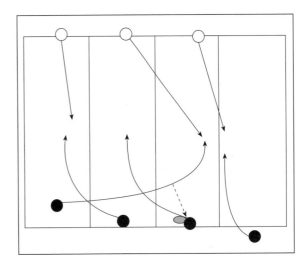

Diagram 10.4 Switch pass.

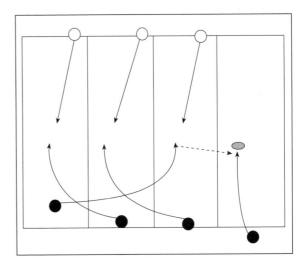

Diagram 10.5 Pass to the outside channel.

a gap in the defence.

However, if you run outward and away from the other attackers, they should run to the same side of their channels so that the subsequent passes do not become too long (see diagram 10.6). Once you have begun to run down the outside edge of your channel,

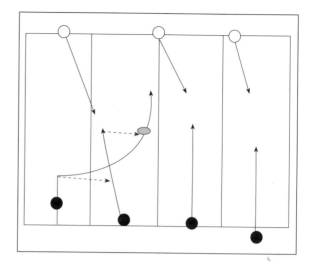

Diagram 10.7 A return loop pass.

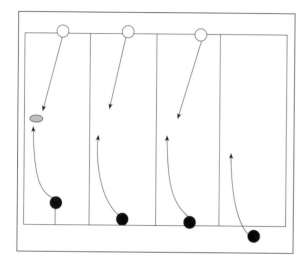

Diagram 10.6 Support and follow ball carrier.

you can pass to another player using any of the passing techniques previously described.

You should now begin to practise a range of other options. You can run toward the support runners, make a pass before leaving your channel and continue to run behind the first pass receiver to take the return loop pass into a gap (see diagram 10.7). If the gap closes, you can make another pass: pop pass outside, flick back inside, miss pass outside and so on.

Adding opposition to the practice and taking away the marked out channels will test whether your unit understands what you are trying to achieve. These are the goals you should focus on:

- Running at a defence as a ball carrier, and delivering the ball safely into a gap in the defence (see diagrams 10.3 and 10.4)
- Running at an angle to the defence to misshape it, then passing to the support runner who is now running at the gap in the misshapen defence (see diagram 10.4)
- Running at an angle to the defence and passing to a support runner who has space around the outside of the defence (see diagram 10.5)

This simple attacking system can be used to attack any organised defence on either side of the ruck or maul, against the mid-field defence from scrums or up the narrow side of the field from the base of a scrum when full back and winger are supporting a penetrative run by the scrum half.

MINI-UNITS SUCCESS STOPPERS

Error	Correction
1. The sequences you practise do not work in the match.	1. Practise only against live opposition once you have learned the basic running and passing patterns of your moves. This is the only way to practise your running lines and timing for entry into the attacking line. If the moves still do not work, you should work on the distance at which your moves take place from your opponents. They may be either too close or too far and the timing of your passes may be either too soon or too late.
2. After your run, your options are reduced.	2. Watch how the support runners react to your running line. Do they run away from you or close down your space? Remind them that they should follow you, remain parallel to the touch lines or fill in the space you have left if you cross into their channel.

MINI-UNITS

DRILLS

1. Basic Attack Skills

Use a set of markers to mark out four channels no wider than 5 metres and no longer than 15 metres. Four players stand one in each channel at one end ready to begin. The ball carrier starts from one of the side channels and should begin the practice by running forward first. The support players then must react to the ball carrier's actions.

When a defender comes into the practice it is the role of the ball carrier to fix the defender to the ball carrying channel by taking up a running line which threatens a score.

Success Goal = 10 out of 10 correct manoeuvres ____

Success Check
• React to ball carrier, but remain parallel to touch lines unless ball carrier crosses channels or runs away from you ____
• Always run at a space in defence, not a player ____

To Increase Difficulty
• Remove channels and add opposition, but always have one more attacker than defenders.
• Add an extra defender, so that there is the same number of defenders and attackers.
• Move the defenders and attackers closer together.

To Decrease Difficulty
• Always have 2 or 3 more attackers than defenders.
• Allow defenders only to jog toward the attackers.

2. Playing Against Defenders

Play 3 vs. 2 in the channel marked out no more than 5 m wide and 20 m long. The coach stands in the first channel and delivers the ball to start the practice. All channels may be used in the attack. The two defenders then select two channels to enter. The attackers must then find the empty channel with the ball using the range of passing options already practised.

Success Goal = 10 out of 10 successful attacks down the empty channel ___

Success Check
• Run hard at the defence ___
• Watch the shape of the defence as you approach it ___
• Use the pass option which best suits the circumstances and gives the ball to the player in the empty channel ___

To Increase Difficulty
• Attacking players start with their backs toward the defence and only turn on the coach's signal.
• Allow defenders to change channels at will.

To Decrease Difficulty
• Defending players start with their backs to the channels and only turn as the attackers receive the ball.

3. 4 vs. 3 in Channels

The attackers have a fourth player who can roam and join in any channel from behind the front three. The attackers must now use the full width of the channels so that space is created for a player attacking from behind them, to find the gap in the defence.

Success Goal = 10 scores out of 10 attempts ___

Success Check
• All players react to the actions of the ball carrier ___
• Play close to the defence so that they cannot shift their defensive formation once the first pass has been made ___
• Fix them in their defensive positions by the speed of your running ___

To Increase Difficulty
• Allow defenders to change channels in order to defend.
• Play down the channels to begin with, then onto an open field with another defender to beat in order to score.

To Decrease Difficulty
• Add another attacker who also attacks from behind.

MINI-UNITS SUCCESS SUMMARY

Teams which have effective mini-units are normally very successful. A strong back row or front row often means that your team monopolises the possession in some area of play. If to these are added a back three who run powerfully in support of a creative mid-field, your team will have many of the ingredients for success. Remember to have another player or coach evaluate your technique and check your progress.

STEP 11

TACTICS AND STRATEGIES: UNDERSTANDING THE GAME

Imagine what it must have felt like to be William Webb Ellis, who in 1823 picked up a ball and ran forward with it during an informal game of football at Rugby School in England. It was William Webb Ellis's instinctive action that created the game of rugby union for you to enjoy. If you have the pace, technique, skill and determination to evade all the defenders who are intent on stopping you, you can go forward at full speed in control of the ball and the game for up to 100 metres. Few other games permit such uninterrupted forward motion.

Usually, however, you will need help from teammates to keep the ball going forward toward your opponent's goal line. Rugby is unique in that to go forward, you have to pass the ball backward. By passing the ball backward, you sometimes create a situation of diminishing returns, because quite a lot of your players can end up in front of the ball in poor support positions (for example, when the backs pass the ball down the line from a line-out or scrum). As a result, many teams may choose to kick the ball to gain ground and go forward. But if the kick is inaccurate, possession is given away, and without the ball you lose control of the game.

Let's think about the game in a little more detail. The better you understand the game, the better your decision-making and playing ability.

Aims and Challenges of the Game

Your prime aim is to score more points than the opposition by carrying the ball over the goal line to score a try and by kicking conversions, drop goals and penalty goals. In attack, you and your team need to answer three questions:

1. How can we keep possession?
2. How can we invade the opposition's territory, get over the tackle line and get behind the gain line and prepare to score?
3. How can we score?

In defence, you and your team need to answer these three questions:

1. How can we win back possession?
2. How can we stop the invasion of our territory?
3. How can we stop the opposition from scoring?

As the ball carrier, you control the game and can decide when or where to pass, kick or run. You will be involved in contests for possession at kick-offs, scrums, line-outs, rucks and mauls, and when fielding kicked balls. It is vital that you and your team master the necessary techniques and skills to win possession of the ball. Having won the ball, you and your team should aim to keep the ball until you ultimately score by mastering your continuity and contact skills. When you have possession of the ball, there is no way that your opponents can score. So be careful not to kick away possession aimlessly.

By having the ability to *win* and *keep* the ball, you establish control for your team and create the opportunity to best *use* the ball. Do you penetrate (run through), outflank (run around) or kick over the opposition? You base these crucial decisions on the shape of the defence in front of you, your position on the field and the closeness and number of support players available. You try to play to your strengths and to probe and exploit the opposition's weaknesses. You of course have to consider other factors, such as the weather, the ground conditions, the referee and the state of play (How long to go? Does your team

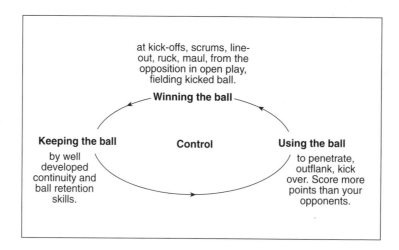

at kick-offs, scrums, line-
out, ruck, maul, from the
opposition in open play,
fielding kicked ball.

— **Winning the ball** —

Keeping the ball   **Control**   **Using the ball**

by well   to penetrate,
developed   outflank, kick
continuity and   over. Score more
ball retention   points than your
skills.   opponents.

Diagram 11.1   Controlling the game.

need to score? Does your team need to hang on to their lead?). Remember that keeping the ball does not necessarily result in pressure, unless you can use it to go forward, beyond the contact point. In general, your forwards are often the "ball getters", and your backs are the "ball users". However, all players on your team should be able both to get and to use the ball.

Principles of Play

You know it is important to establish control of the game. Control can be achieved only if you understand and enact the following four principles of play:

1. Going forward
2. Support
3. Continuity
4. Pressure

Going Forward

These are the keys to success in going forward:

- Run straight toward the goal line parallel to touch lines rather than across the field toward the touch lines. Understand why this is needed.
- Strive to get a ball carrier in front of the rest of your team, over the gain line or beyond the tackle line, to break the first line of defence and enable your attackers to run at a retreating defence.

- Tempt defenders to bunch up in one area of the field so that attacking space is created elsewhere for your distributors and play makers to enable your penetrators and support runners to go forward at pace.
- Score a try.

There are various ways for you to achieve these keys to success. For example, your forwards could retain possession and keep driving forward, sucking in the opposition, then deliver the ball to your backs to run at retreating defenders. A quickly executed number 8 pick-up at the base of the scrum is one way of getting a ball carrier over the gain line quickly, as is a line-out peel and drive. Your backs will attempt to go forward with purpose, by accurate passing and skilful running and evasion or by kicking over the defence and chasing. You need to be able to carry the ball forward and, when necessary, pass to a teammate who is better placed to carry the ball beyond you.

Support

In any rugby game you may handle the ball for less than 2 minutes. So what are you expected to do for the other 78 minutes of the game? When you are not handling the ball, you play a major or minor supporting role in either attack or defence, to maximise the use of possession for your team. You need to be fit enough to run for most of the game. Good support is not accidental, it is deliberate; your team needs to develop good communication channels so you know where and when to run in support of whatever team ploy is being executed in a particular area of the field.

If you are within 10 metres of the ball carrier, you should know what is happening and be ready to act and react. If you are within 5 metres of the ball, you are involved in the action and can influence the outcome by being available for support and giving the ball carrier more options. If you are within 1 metre of the ball carrier, you must already have made your decision and be directly involved in the action.

These are the keys to success in support:

- As the ball carrier, you are unlikely to beat all the defenders, so you must assess how far to go and how and when to use the available support.
- As the ball carrier, you need support on both sides to maximise your choices and make defence difficult. One of your support runners should run parallel to the touch lines to keep the ball going forward if he or she receives it and possibly to outflank the defence.
- As a support runner, you need to keep some depth directly behind the ball carrier so you can decide at the last minute which space is best to attack: left, right or straight ahead. Perfect timing of your run is vital to add momentum to the attack.
- You should be prepared to run positively in support all game. You won't always receive the ball, but you can be an important decoy runner. If at first you don't receive the ball, try, try again, because ultimately you will score a try.
- Good support play is vital when your team are contesting for possession and are in close physical contact. For example, line-out jumpers need to be supported in the air for safety reasons, and supporters need to hold up teammates in rucks and mauls so that they stay on their feet and keep driving forward.

Continuity

Your aim is to maintain controlled continuity and control of the ball until your team scores. You attempt to sustain your attack despite the efforts of the defenders to halt it. As a ball carrier, you time your pass to a receiver so that you both avoid contact and the support runner can carry the ball forward into space. In reality you need to use your contact techniques to protect and recycle possession (use the ball again) during temporary stoppages to your forward movement (rucks or mauls).

This is a typical passage of continuous play: Attack first against an organised, formal defence from line-out or scrum ball. If stopped, recycle the ball quickly from a ruck or maul. Launch a second attack at a more disorganised defence. If halted again, recycle the ball under control quickly, and attack again through the gaps of a now scattered defence.

Attempt to keep the ball alive and move it around quickly, constantly changing the focus of attack and weakening the defence so someone is out of position, until you create a situation where your attackers outnumber defenders and you have adequate space in which to move forward. Your success will be based on how many good decisions you make.

To succeed at continuity requires that players possess these skills and attributes:

- Ball-handling and retention skills to keep the ball under control in contact and tackle situations
- Quick decision-making abilities
- Well-timed support skills by close- and wide-running players
- Play with head up to choose accurately where the ball can be best used next

Pressure

Exert sustained pressure on your opponents in attack and defence to force them to make mistakes from which points can be scored. You should attempt to deny your opponents space in which to play and time to think and act. If your team can get a ball carrier over the gain line and in behind the opposition's defence, can support in numbers and can establish controlled continuity, your opponents will have difficulty dealing with the pressure this causes.

These are the keys to success of pressure *in attack*:

- Attack opposition's weaknesses.
- Keep possession, and produce and use good, quick ball.
- Eliminate mistakes such as handling errors.
- Keep the ball alive, and change your focus of attack.
- Put the ball behind opposition by getting over the gain line and chasing kicks well to maintain possession.
- Force the defence to bunch up in one area of the field, then quickly attack the spaces being poorly covered by a disorganised or scattered defence.

These are the keys to success of pressure *in defence:*

- Deny the opposition space to act and time to think.
- Close down the space between you fast to force errors by the ball carrier.
- Tackle your opponents as far behind the gain line as possible. Attempt to drive your opponents backward in the tackle and dislodge the ball to reclaim possession.
- Attack the ball carrier; disrupt and halt opposition's attempts to retain and recycle the ball in rucks and mauls. Slow the ball down until you recover possession.
- Organise your defence to cover all possible attacking tactics by recovering your defensive positions quickly.
- Attack your opposition at scrum, line-out, ruck and maul to make it difficult for them to use good, controlled ball.
- Be hungry to reclaim the ball, and hunt for it in numbers.

Decision Making and Using the Ball

As you play the game, you need to respond to the constantly changing situations that confront you. You will find yourself adapting to the actions and reactions of your own team and the opposition. The game changes very quickly, and your ability to cope depends largely on your understanding of the situation you and your teammates face. Moreover, you need to understand each other and read the game in the same way to be effective. You will be faced by various challenges in attack and defence, when you are carrying the ball and when you're not. You will have a split second to answer certain questions and to react purposefully, as shown for example in diagram 11.2.

As the ball carrier or a player involved in the action, you should ask yourself three questions: What is happening? What decision do I make? What skill do I choose to achieve my aim? You need to get used

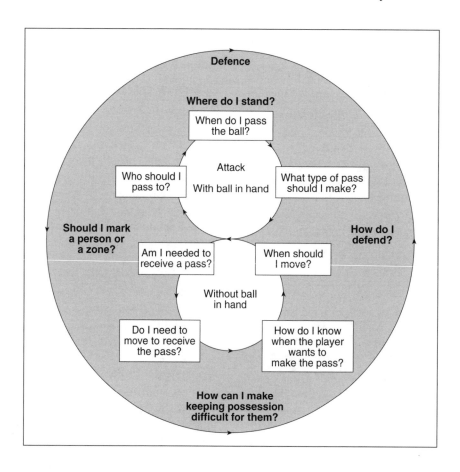

Diagram 11.2 Understanding your role in attack and defence.

to experiencing the decision-making sequence of *see, understand, decide, act.*

Look up and scan the positioning of the opposition and your teammates. Understand the possible options and outcomes. Decide what course of action to take. Then act on your decision. All this, of course, must happen in an instant, and your ability and understanding of the game will be put to the test. You need two levels of understanding. First, you must understand the game well enough to decide on your action. Then, as a result of your action, you should better understand your involvement and the outcome to assess how well you understood in the first place.

If your action worked, you can store it in your repertoire of responses and try it again next time. If you misunderstood the situation and your subsequent action failed, you will need to think again, change and adapt accordingly. Your decision-making cycle will then become: see, understand, decide, act, better understand.

Diagrams 11.3 and 11.4 demonstrate two possible decision-making sequences, in attack when using the ball to score (diagram 11.3) and in defence when you are trying to stop the opposition from scoring (diagram 11.4). Every player in your team is a decision maker and will have to decide how

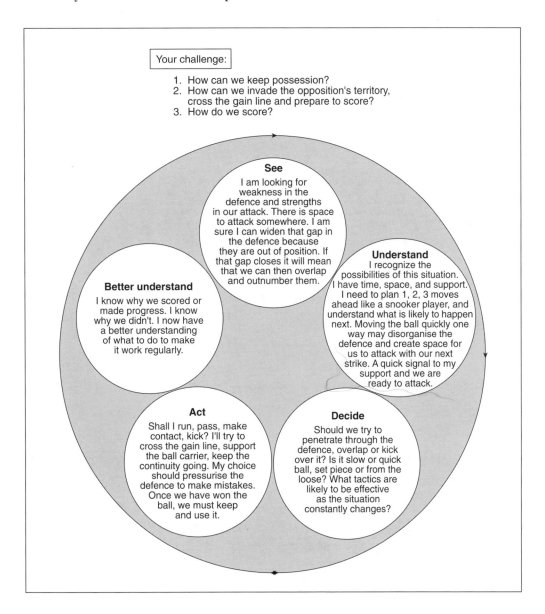

Diagram 11.3 Thinking about how to attack the opposition.

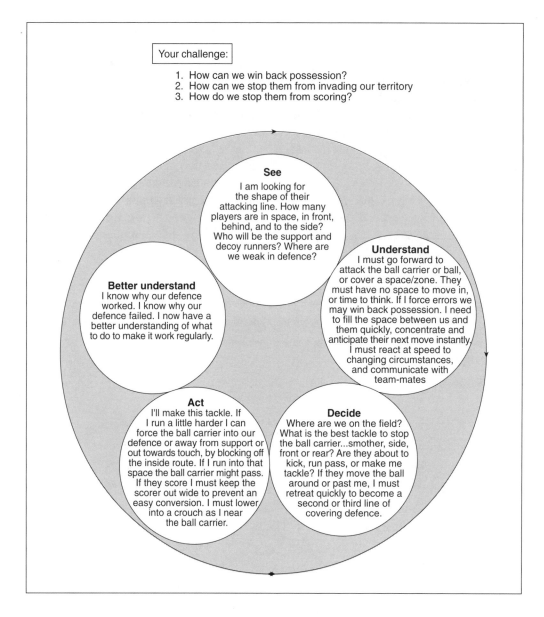

Your challenge:

1. How can we win back possession?
2. How can we stop them from invading our territory
3. How do we stop them from scoring?

See

I am looking for the shape of their attacking line. How many players are in space, in front, behind, and to the side? Who will be the support and decoy runners? Where are we weak in defence?

Understand

I must go forward to attack the ball carrier or ball, or cover a space/zone. They must have no space to move in, or time to think. If I force errors we may win back possession. I need to fill the space between us and them quickly, concentrate and anticipate their next move instantly. I must react at speed to changing circumstances, and communicate with team-mates

Better understand

I know why our defence worked. I know why our defence failed. I now have a better understanding of what to do to make it work regularly.

Act

I'll make this tackle. If I run a little harder I can force the ball carrier into our defence or away from support or out towards touch, by blocking off the inside route. If I run into that space the ball carrier might pass. If they score I must keep the scorer out wide to prevent an easy conversion. I must lower into a crouch as I near the ball carrier.

Decide

Where are we on the field? What is the best tackle to stop the ball carrier...smother, side, front or rear? Are they about to kick, run pass, or make me tackle? If they move the ball around or past me, I must retreat quickly to become a second or third line of covering defence.

Diagram 11.4 Thinking about how to stop the opposition.

best to use the ball in a number of different situations.

To create space for your team and overcome a defence, you will be involved in making tactical decisions to optimise the way you use the ball in your attempts to score. There are three basic tactics to beat a defence, chosen in response to the shape of the defence in front of you: You can pull the defence wide and penetrate it, pull it close together and outflank it or pull it forward and kick the ball over it.

If you are faced with a defence shaped like the one in diagram 11.5, you could attempt to penetrate it by using a decoy runner to attract the attention of

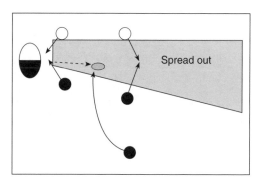

Spread out

Diagram 11.5 Penetrate a spread-out defence.

the defence away from the passer, who gives a short pass to the penetrating runner. Close, instant support is required for the penetrator, who needs to run strongly and have good ball retention abilities.

If you are faced with a defence shaped like the one in diagram 11.6, you could attempt to outflank it by stopping your players running toward the space and encouraging them "by talking" to use running lines that hold the defence away from the space. You need good, quick accurate handling to release a pass to a support player at pace, such as the blind-side wing or full back, who can then run into and through the unoccupied space.

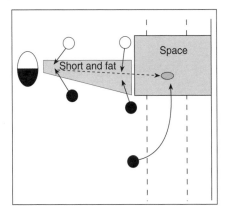

Diagram 11.6   Outflank a tight defence.

If you are faced with a long, thin, fast-approaching defence as in diagram 11.7, you may decide to kick into the space behind it. Your kick must be accurate, and your chasers must have a good chance of regaining possession.

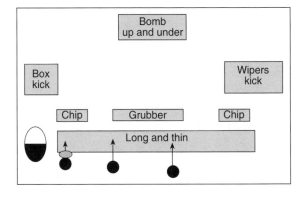

Diagram 11.7   Kick over a fast-approaching defence.

Developing Tactics and Strategies

You should have a purpose for all the support running you do in a game. You need to devise a plan and know what your team may attempt in different positions and areas on the pitch. The full-sized pitch is approximately 100 metres long from goal line to goal line and approximately 70 metres wide from sideline to sideline. Much of your game is like doing a jig-saw puzzle: piecing bits together until you finally have the full picture and know how to score a try. You play in one part of the pitch, move the ball, then start again. You develop a pattern in the way you use and create space for each other. A scrum or a line-out brings 16 to 18 players close together, leaving a lot of space on either side for the remaining 12 players to attack and defend.

To help you create a framework for your team, you could divide the field up into zones and create an overall view of how you might play in each area (see diagram 11.8).

It's important for you not to be stifled by your plan, but to be confident to adapt, improvise and play to what you see in front of you. If you are in your own 22-metre area and there is space in front of you, have a go! Some of the best tries are scored from deep in your 22-metre area, because the opposition do not expect you to run with the ball, have often lost some of their concentration and left gaps in their defence. So look to maximise your strengths and exploit the opposition's weaknesses, which may mean adapting your plan before and during the game.

To move the ball forward and score, you need to think and act much more quickly than the opposition. All your teammates need to communicate with each other at stoppages and as the game is in motion to ensure that you get more players near the ball than the opposition, keep the ball and remain in control of the game.

In addition to a plan of action for various zones up the length of the pitch, it's a good idea to have a similar understanding of what may happen in channels going across the pitch. With a map of the field like the one in diagram 11.9, you can communicate precisely where you intend to move the ball and get an idea of who can support the ball and where the ball can be supported by most of your players. You can create a grid reference system by combining the

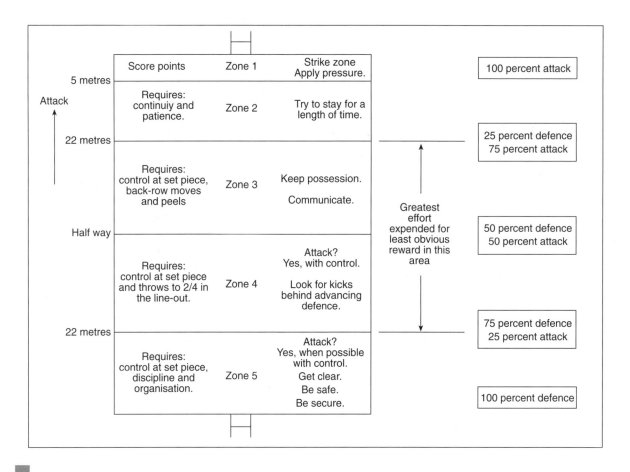

		100 percent attack
Score points	Zone 1	Strike zone Apply pressure.
Requires: continuiy and patience.	Zone 2	Try to stay for a length of time.
		25 percent defence 75 percent attack
Requires: control at set piece, back-row moves and peels	Zone 3	Keep possession. Communicate.
		50 percent defence 50 percent attack
Requires: control at set piece and throws to 2/4 in the line-out.	Zone 4	Attack? Yes, with control. Look for kicks behind advancing defence.
		75 percent defence 25 percent attack
Requires: control at set piece, discipline and organisation.	Zone 5	Attack? Yes, when possible with control. Get clear. Be safe. Be secure.
		100 percent defence

5 metres — Attack ↑ — 22 metres — Half way — 22 metres

Greatest effort expended for least obvious reward in this area

Diagram 11.8   Creating a playing framework.

zones of diagram 11.8 with the channels of diagram 11.9. After winning the ball at a line-out in zone 3, channel A, you could indicate that you wish to move the ball by passing quickly by hand to zone 2, channel D.

If you have a scrum in zone 3, channel A, and decide to move the ball down the blind or narrow side in this 17-18 metre wide channel, you can get 12 players in support of the ball quickly: all 8 forwards, left winger, scrum half, fly half and inside centre. If you win the ball in channel A and move it to channel B, you could get eight support players involved quickly to keep the ball moving forward. If you aim to do something in channel C, six support players would be readily available, and in channel D you could probably get four players in good support positions. But how will the opposition react? If all your players know what is likely to happen, hopefully they will arrive

first, act quickly, keep the defence guessing and highlight the opposition's weaknesses.

Before your players go down in a scrum or get to a line-out, you should all know what you might do with the ball next. For example, you may move the ball quickly from channel A to B, where your centre and flanker link up to recycle and reuse the ball, so that you can then attack the blind side you created back in channel A by moving the defence across into channel B with your first play. The blind side is often the least defended area of the field.

As your team develops understanding, you can better put various bits and pieces of play together in your attempts to confuse and scatter the opposition's defence. Once you have developed a framework, it will be easier for your team to play with confidence. You will be able to demonstrate that you understand the game.

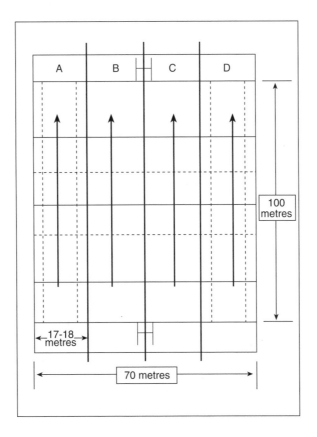

Diagram 11.9   Identifying the playing zones/channels.

TACTICS AND STRATEGIES SUCCESS SUMMARY

By understanding the game, and practising your techniques, you will become a skilful and intelligent performer, who can also deal with unpredictable situations during a game.

In your attempts to go forward up the pitch, you will need to overcome the challenge of having to play a lateral game, where you pass the ball sideways or backwards, in order to go forward. Some of the starting points of the game are dictated, and more predictable, like scrums, line-outs and restarts. Your challenge is to be unpredictable and spontaneous, and to understand what best to do between these set pieces.

At each point during the game, you and your team will be continually making choices about what to do next. At set pieces like scrums, you will be aware of the various tactical possibilities, and make a choice before the action starts, and during the action. Each new decision is in the hands of the different player with the ball, and you must react to the new decision, and change your actions accordingly. You need to weigh up the possibilities around you, and recognise gaps and spaces to attack. For example, if the defence in front of you is spread, then you could penetrate it, and when the defence is bunched together, you could move the ball wide and outflank it.

It is important to remember that you will not go forward effectively unless you understand gain and tackle line principles. You will not have support unless the non-ball carriers appreciate lines of support running. You will not achieve continuity until you manage the contact area well, and you will not put pressure on the opposition unless you put pressure on yourself.

At the end of each practice and game ask yourself the following questions:

"Did I really understand what I was trying to do?"

"Did I appreciate all the possible outcomes of each piece of play?"

"Did I read my teammates' body language and support them effectively?"

"Did I try to create space for myself and my teammates?"

"Did I run at space and gaps rather than at people?"

"Did I consider releasing the ball before contact?"

"Did I know how to disorganise the opposition's defence?"

"Did I sense what was happening 1m, 5m, 10m, 15m, 30m away from me, sideways, behind and in front?"

"Did I have the ability to go forward under control to cross the gain and tackle lines (see diagram 11.10), keep the ball, play fast and slow when needed, move the defence around and score as a result of considered action, rather than by chance?"

You will learn from your experiences, so that your decision-making sequence of thought becomes see, understand, decide, act, better understand. You will learn from your mistakes and successes, and adapt accordingly.

Maybe one day like William Webb Ellis you will do something instinctive in the game that no-one else has done before, and take the game forward with a new technique or idea for others to attempt to imitate and understand. There is always something new to understand and learn. Keep enjoying your rugby; and "Think even when you blink".

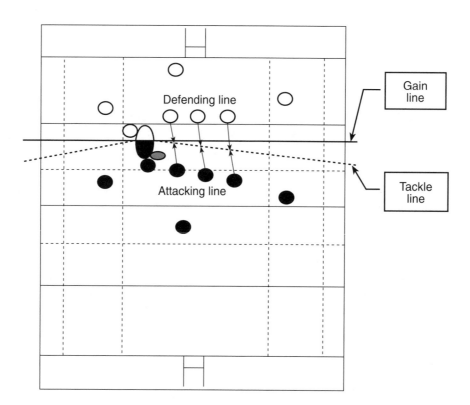

Diagram 11.10 Crossing the gain and tackle lines.

RATING YOUR PROGRESS

Rugby competence equals rugby skills plus rugby knowledge plus application in a variety of practice and game situations.

You have been learning and practising a wide range of techniques and movements and developing your understanding of rugby. Once you have mastered a rugby technique and can perform it regularly and successfully against live opposition, it becomes a rugby skill. At this stage in your rugby development, it's important to ask yourself three questions:

- What have I achieved?
- What do I have to do to improve?
- Who can I ask to help me improve?

To help your development as a player, it is a good idea to self-assess your ability and knowledge and to reflect on your experiences. This gives you a feeling of increased involvement in your rugby learning process. You should set yourself some short-term and long-term objectives. You need to recognise your strengths and weaknesses; practise the skills needed to improve both, but especially your weaknesses. Even international players are guilty of spending too much time practising what they are already good at and ignoring their weaknesses.

If you require more feedback to help you improve, ask a friend to observe you playing and to make some simple notes, for example, the number of tackles, passes and kicks you make in the game. You also need to know the outcomes of your actions and whether they were successful or not. For example, was your passing accurate enough to create space or time for the receiver? Did you select the best kind of pass for the situation, and did the pass give other options to the receiver?

If you are lucky enough to have a video camera available, have a friend film you either practising or playing in a game. Watching yourself in action can provide you with more information about your skill level and the outcomes of your actions.

Your self-assessment process should provide you with feedback and feed-forward. The following charts are intended to help you assess the quality of your performance. Many of the criteria refer to the general skills each player requires to be successful in the team. However, there are some rather more specialised charts that you should consult if, for example, you are one of the tactical kickers.

Use a rating that best reflects your progress to date in the various rugby skills. "Very good" (VG) means that you have the ability to perform well consistently, not only in practice, but more important, in a game. "Good" (G) means that you are satisfied that the majority of the time (at least 7 out of 10 times) you perform well in practice and during matches. If you mark "needs developing" (ND), you feel that you are currently unable to perform the activity with any certainty: you perform poorly as often as well at that skill. If you mark "needs significant development" (SD), you feel you need further in-depth teaching and practice to improve your performance in the activity. It's a good idea to keep a notebook with a section titled "I need further help to develop my . . ."

You might wish to keep the charts as a portfolio of achievement so that you are aware of the rate of your improvement. Copy the charts and date them when you progress from one rating to the next.

So, how do you think you rate in the following rugby skills?

Rating Your Progress

Passing, Receiving and Evasive Running: Refer to Steps 2 and 3

Lateral pass (sideways), right hand ____
Lateral pass (sideways), left hand ____
Switch pass off right hand ____
Switch pass off left hand ____
Loop pass off right hand ____
Loop pass off left hand ____
Miss (skip over) pass off right hand ____
Miss (skip over) pass off left hand ____
Receiving passes from the right ____
Receiving passes from the left ____

2 vs. 1 attack to the right ____
2 vs. 1 attack to the left ____
3 vs. 2 attack to the right ____
3 vs. 2 attack to the left ____
Change of pace ____
Swerve to right ____
Swerve to left ____
Sidestep from right leg ____
Sidestep from left leg ____

Tackling: Refer to Step 4

Tackling from side, right shoulder ____
Tackling from side, left shoulder ____
Tackling from front, right shoulder ____

Tackling from front, left shoulder ____
Tackling from rear, right shoulder ____
Tackling from rear, left shoulder ____

Kicking: Refer to Step 5

Punt for distance and accuracy, right foot ____
Punt for distance and accuracy, left foot ____
Punt for height, right foot ____
Punt for height, left foot ____
Grubber kick, right foot ____
Grubber kick, left foot ____
Box kick, right foot ____
Box kick, left foot ____

Wipers kick, right foot ____
Wipers kick, left foot ____
Drop kick, right foot ____
Drop kick, left foot ____
Chip kick, right foot ____
Chip kick, left foot ____
Kick at goal ____
Kick-off ____
22-metre drop-out ____

Contact: Refer to Step 6

Falling to the ground under control ____
Bump and pass ____
Bump and roll ____
Bump, roll and gut pass ____
Placing the ball on the ground for the ruck ____

Support in the ruck ____
Setting up the ball standing for the maul ____
Support in the maul ____
Regaining feet quickly to rejoin the game ____

There are a number of people who can help you develop as a player. Your coach may want to assess your playing ability using the preceding rating charts in order to design a development programme for you. The purpose of such assessments is to help you develop your skills by identifying your current strengths and weaknesses.

To help you improve your physical and individual skills, you will also need to follow a fitness programme incorporating health, skill and ability related components. As you develop your fitness, you will find that you are able to perform your skills to a high standard throughout the game and should make fewer mistakes. That difficult pass near your feet will be picked up, and you will dive over in the corner to score the match-winning try.

As your skill and fitness levels develop, your improved understanding of the game will help you to more often make good decisions during a match. You can improve your understanding of rugby by playing, watching, talking about and reading about the game.

How well do you understand the game?

Understanding the Game: Refer to Step 11

Understanding the principles of
  play ____

Understanding tactics ____

Scanning for opportunities ____

Option choosing ____

Decision making ____

Communication ____

Anticipation ____

Reaction to changing situations ____

Your attitude is as important as your understanding and physical skills. The following chart on personal qualities will help you to decide how you respond to instructions, whether you are willing to learn and how you relate to other players in your squad. Although the following chart is for your own use, it is often a good idea to let a friend or your coach fill it out too. You will then have a more complete picture of how you relate to the others in the squad.

Personal Qualities

Ability to work in a team ____

Unselfishness ____

Encouraging others ____

Fair play ____

Good sportsmanship ____

Confidence ____

Relationship with coach ____

Watching demonstrations closely ____

Listening carefully to instructions ____

Wearing the correct kilt ____

Self-control in unstructured
  situations ____

Overall progress as a rugby player ____

The purpose of all this assessment is to make sure that help is available so you can develop into an all-round rugby player who has the skills to perform successfully against any other player and who enjoys playing the game. Enjoy your rugby.

GLOSSARY

advantage—When the non-offending team, following an infringement, takes the opportunity to develop play and gains some of their opponent's territory (a tactical advantage) or scores.

agility—The ability to move quickly from one position to another, for example, moving from the ground to your feet or nimbly changing your direction of running.

attack—The action of the team in possession of the ball who are trying to score.

back five—Players who wear numbers 11 to 15. They are five of the players generally known as the backs (together with the scrum half and fly half).

back row—Players who normally wear numbers 6 to 8 (the two flankers and number 8) whose role it is to destroy the opposition's attacks and create opportunities in attack for their own team.

backs (also known as three-quarters)—The players who normally wear numbers 9 to 15 and play outside the scrummage and line-out.

back three—Players who normally wear numbers 11, 14 and 15 and whose role is to defend against kicks, initiate any possible counter-attacks and act as strike runners in support of the mid-field attack.

ball carrier—The person carrying the ball.

bind—To wrap arms around other players and grip tightly. Players normally bind in scrummages, rucks, mauls, and line-outs.

blind side—The narrow side of the field between the set piece/ruck/maul, usually the area with least defenders.

body composition—The relative proportions of muscle, bone, fat and other vital parts in the body.

box kick—A punt, normally by either scrum half or fly half, that flies high over and beyond a scrummage or line-out for teammates to chase.

breakdown—The moment in time when a sequence of activity (passing, running in attack, etc.) stops due to the actions of the defence or the inability of the attack to maintain continuity.

centre—The player who makes space for the winger

channel—A narrow practice area or a relatively narrow strip of pitch running up and down the playing field.

chip kick—A kick that floats just over and behind a close opponent for either the kicker or a teammate to catch.

continuity—Maintaining possession through a series of phases of play.

conversion—A kick at goal after a try has been scored.

dead ball—A ball becomes dead when the referee blows his or her whistle to indicate a stoppage of play or when an attempt to convert a try is unsuccessful.

defence—The actions of the team without the ball, who are trying to prevent the opposition from scoring.

drift defence—A type of defence used by backs, who gradually move from the immediate opponent to tackle one or more players farther out. Drift defence can happen only if the attackers pass the ball too early or run at an angle toward the touch line.

drive—To bind together and push opponents back; to run powerfully in a close group toward the opponents' goal line. An action normally associated with forwards.

drop goal—A drop kick that crosses over the crossbar and between the goal posts to score 3 points.

drop kick—A kick in which the kicker drops the ball point first and kicks it as it makes contact with the ground.

drop-out—A drop kick awarded to the defending team that may be taken anywhere along or behind the 22-metre line once the ball has been made dead by the defence in the in-goal area.

dummy pass—A way of fooling the defence by setting up to pass, going through the passing movement but retaining the ball.

fair catch (mark)—A defender makes a fair catch (mark), when in the 22-metre or in-goal area, cleanly catches the ball direct from an opponent's kick (other than kick-off) and at the same time calls "Mark!". A fair catch may be made even though the ball on its way touches a goal post or crossbar.

field of play—The area between the goal lines and touch lines. The lines are not part of the field of play. See also playing area.

first 5/8th—The Southern Hemisphere name for the fly half.

flanker—The player who wears number 6 or 7 who acts as a link and continuity player between the backs and forwards in attack and defence.

flexibility—Increased joint mobility, that helps to prevent injury. Flexibility is improved by stretching the muscles and connective tissue around a joint.

fly half—A key decision maker in the team who wears number 10. This player is the key tactician who receives possession from the forwards via the scrum half.

forward pass—A pass that travels toward your opponent's goal line which results in a scrummage or counter-attacking opportunity to your opponents.

forwards—The players who normally wear numbers 1 to 8 and who take part in scrummages and line-outs.

foul play—Any action by a player that is contrary to the letter and spirit of the game, including obstruction, unfair play, misconduct, dangerous play, unsporting behaviour, retaliation and repeated infringements.

free kick—A kick awarded for a fair catch or to the non-offending team as stated in the laws of the game. A goal may not be scored from the free kick.

front five—Players who wear numbers 1 to 5 and who occupy the front row and the middle two positions of the second row in the scrummage.

front row—Players who wear the numbers 1, 2 or 3 and who make direct contact with the opposition at each scrummage.

full back—The player who normally wears number 15, is usually the last line of defence and is used as a penetrative runner in attack.

gain line—An imaginary line between the two teams designating the line that the attacking players would need to reach in order for the ball to be ahead of the forwards.

grubber kick—A kick that is deliberately struck so that it rolls along the ground.

gut pass—A pass that does not leave the passer's hands until the ball is pushed up and into the receiver's midriff; normally used by forwards in close contact situations.

half backs—The collective name for the scrum half and fly half.

hooker—The player who normally wears number 2, whose roles usually include throwing the ball into the line-out and hooking the ball back in the scrummages.

infringement—An action that violates the laws of the game.

in-goal—The area between the goal line and the dead-ball line and between the touch-in-goal lines. It includes the goal line but not the others.

inside—The direction or place from which the ball has just been passed away from the forwards.

infield—The position away from the touch line and toward the centre of the field.

inside centre—The centre playing next to the fly half.

International Rugby Football Board (IRFB)—The association of national Rugby Football Unions, whose role is to promote, foster and extend the game and to alter and develop the laws of the game.

kick—A kick is made by striking the ball with any part of the foot (except the heel) or leg from toe to knee, including the knee.

kick-off—(a) A place kick taken from the centre of the half-way line by the team that has the right to start the match or by the opposing team after the half-time interval. (b) A drop kick taken at or from behind the centre of the half-way line by the defending team after the opposing side has scored.

knock-on (throw forward)—A knock-on occurs when the ball travels toward the direction of the opponent's dead-ball line after a player loses possession of it; a player strikes or propels it with the hand or arm; or it strikes a player's hand or arm and touches the ground or another player before it is recovered by the player.

lay-off pass—A soft pass into the space created by the ball carrier.

line of touch—The imaginary line at right angles to the touch line at the place where the ball is thrown in from touch.

line-out—A formation of at least two players from each team lined up in single lines, parallel to the line of touch (i.e., at right angles to the touch line) in readiness for the ball to be thrown in between them after the ball has gone into touch.

lock—A player who usually wears number 4 or 5, plays in the middle row of the scrummage, jumps for the ball in the line-out and at kick-off situations..

loop pass—A pass that puts the receiver into a space in the defence. The receiver has normally just passed the ball and run around and behind the ball carrier to receive the return loop pass.

loose forwards (loosies)—A Southern Hemisphere name for the back row.

loose-head prop—The player who wears number 1, packs on the left-hand side of the front row, supports the jumper in the jump-and-catch sequence in the line-out and at kick-offs.

mark—The place where a free kick or penalty is awarded. See also fair catch.

maul—A formation, which can take place only in the field of play, of one or more players from each team on their feet and in physical contact closing around the player who is in possession of the ball.

middle five—The half backs and back row forwards.

mid-field—(a) The fly half and two centres. (b) The middle of the playing field.

miss pass—A lateral pass which deliberately misses out one or more support players in order to reach a player more appropriately positioned to make best use of the ball.

no side—The end of the match.

number 8—The player who wears number 8, normally packs down in the third row of the scrum and is usually the extra jumper at the rear of the line-out.

offside—In general play, when a player is in front of the ball after it has last been played by another player of the same team; from a set piece or ruck/maul, when player remains or advances in front of the hindmost feet and at line-out if a player advances within 10-metres of the line of touch before the line-out is ended.

onside—Means a player is in the game and not liable to penalty for offside.

out of play—When the ball has gone into touch or touch-in-goal or has touched or crossed the dead-ball line.

outside centre—The centre normally wears 12 or 13 and always plays next to the winger on either side of the field.

overlap—An attacking sequence that normally results in attackers outnumbering the defenders and leads to an attack around the defence.

pass—The movement of the ball from one player's hands to another's.

peel—The act of collecting the ball from the back of a line-out and driving around the end toward the mid-field, normally done by the forwards.

penalty kick—A kick awarded to the non-offending team as stated in the laws of the game. A player may take a kick at goal from a penalty kick.

pitch—Another term used to describe the playing area or playing field.

place kick—Kicking the ball from the ground after it has been placed there for that purpose.

playing area—The field of play and the in-goal areas. The lines are not part of the playing area. (See diagram 1 in the introduction.)

pop pass—A soft, floated pass that flies slightly upward into space in front of the receiver.

possession—When a team or player has the ball under control.

principles of play—The general strategy of how to play the game: going forward, support, continuity and pressure.

punt—A kick in which the player deliberately drops the ball and strikes it before it touches the ground.

put-in—The act of the scrum half putting the ball into the scrummage conforming to the Laws of the game.

recycle—Maintaining and using possession after making contact with the opposition.

referee—The official who keeps the time and score and applies the laws during a match.

roll—Planting the foot firmly at the point of contact and then pivoting around this point to spin out of the contact area.

ruck—A formation, which can take place only in the field of play, of one or more players from each team on their feet and in physical contact closing around the ball on the ground between them.

running line—The direction a player runs in either attack or defence.

screen pass—A pass that uses the passer's body as a screen to prevent the defence from seeing the pass being made, normally used by forwards in contact situations, very similar to the gut pass.

scrum half—Wears number 9 and acts as the link between the forwards and backs.

scrummage (scrum)—A formation, which can take place only in the field of play, of eight players from each team closing up in readiness to allow the ball to be put on the ground between them. It is used to restart the game after an infringement.

second 5/8th—The Southern Hemisphere name for the inside centre.

second row—Players who wear numbers 4, 5, 6 and 7 and form the second line of players in the scrummage, behind the front row.

set piece—A general term used to describe a scrum or line-out formation.

sidestep—A sudden change of forward direction by the ball carrier to run past a defender.

spin pass—A pass that spirals as it flies. Normally used by scrum halves but may also be used by other players, for speed, length and accuracy.

sprigs—The Southern Hemisphere name for studs.

strategy—The playing plan a team adopts to make best use of its strengths and the opposition's weaknesses.

strike runners—Players who run into space and attempt to score.

studs—Alloy or rubber attachments to the soles of boots to assist grip. Studs must conform to the regulations contained in the laws of the game.

swerve—A running line that takes the ball carrier toward a defender and then arcs quickly away from an attempted tackle.

switch pass—A pass that hides the ball from the opposition and changes the direction of the attack.

tackle—When a player carrying the ball in the field of play is held by one or more opponents so that, while held, the player is brought to the ground or the ball comes into contact with the ground.

tackle line—An imaginary line between the two teams drawn along the points at which the attack and defence would meet if they all ran toward each other.

tactics—The way a team plays during a match taking into account the influence of the weather, opponents, referee and other factors that might influence play.

tag rugby—A non-contact form of rugby that replaces the tackle with the removal of a ribbon from the ball carrier.

three-quarter line—Formation and alignment of the backs.

three-quarters—See backs.

throw forward—See knock-on.

throw-in—Throwing the ball into the line-out from touch.

tight-head prop—The player who wears number 3, packs on the right-hand side of the front row, supports the jumper in the jump-and-catch sequence in the line-out and at kick-offs.

touch—The state of the ball when, while not being carried by a player, it touches a touch line or the ground, a person or an object on or beyond the touch line, or when a player who is carrying it touches a touch line or the ground beyond it. At this point the ball is out of play.

touch-in-goal line—The extension of the touch line from corner flag to dead-ball line.

touch line—The line which defines the side of the field of play and runs the length of the field from corner flag to corner flag.

touch rugby—A non-contact form of rugby that replaces the tackle with a two-handed touch.

try (touchdown)—The grounding of the ball in the defending team's in-goal area by a player of the opposing team who is holding the ball in his or her hands or arms, who is exerting downward pressure on the ball with hand(s) or arm(s) while it is on the ground, or who falls on the ball so that it is anywhere under the front of the body, between waist and neck inclusive.

union—The controlling body under whose jurisdiction the match is played.

winger—The player who normally wears either 11 (left wing) or 14 (right wing), is normally on the end of the three-quarter line and is usually one of the fastest players on the team.

wipers kick—A kick that travels diagonally from one side of the playing field to the other, crossing over and behind the opponent's defence to land behind the far winger and roll toward the corner.

zone defence—A form of defence in which a player defends an area on the field and tackles any ball carrier who runs into that space.

About the Authors

Tony Biscombe has more than 25 years of Rugby Union coaching experience. As a member of staff of the Rugby Football Union (RFU), his assignments have included coaching in France, New Zealand, Zimbabwe, Japan, the West Indies, and Germany. In his current role as Divisional Technical Administrator for the RFU, Biscombe evaluates coaches working at all levels of the Game, helps to develop elite youth players and provides technical support and resources for the England team.

Tony Biscombe lives in Leeds, England, with his wife, Larraine, and their two children, James and Zoe. Biscombe enjoys sports in general, golf in particular, and gardening with his wife.

Peter Drewett was a physical education, exercise, and sports science lecturer at the University of Exeter. He is an RFU Senior Coach and also the RFU National Student Development Officer. He has played and coached rugby at various club, county, divisional, and international levels and has coached players ranging from those in school to senior internationals. With Tony Biscombe, Drewett developed the "Supercoach" CD-ROM: a rugby teaching and coaching aid, the first software package of its kind and one that has been praised for both its content and its design.

Drewett's home is in Exeter, England. In his leisure time Drewett enjoys exercising to stay fit and healthy, and having fun with his children, Tom, Oliver and Megan.